The Gulag: A Very Short Introduction

VERY SHORT INTRODUCTIONS are for anyone wanting a stimulating and accessible way into a new subject. They are written by experts, and have been translated into more than 45 different languages.

The series began in 1995, and now covers a wide variety of topics in every discipline. The VSI library currently contains over 750 volumes—a Very Short Introduction to everything from Psychology and Philosophy of Science to American History and Relativity—and continues to grow in every subject area.

Very Short Introductions available now:

ABOLITIONISM Richard S. Newman
THE ABRAHAMIC RELIGIONS
    Charles L. Cohen
ACCOUNTING Christopher Nobes
ADDICTION Keith Humphreys
ADOLESCENCE Peter K. Smith
THEODOR W. ADORNO
    Andrew Bowie
ADVERTISING Winston Fletcher
AERIAL WARFARE Frank Ledwidge
AESTHETICS Bence Nanay
AFRICAN AMERICAN HISTORY
    Jonathan Scott Holloway
AFRICAN AMERICAN RELIGION
    Eddie S. Glaude Jr.
AFRICAN HISTORY John Parker and
    Richard Rathbone
AFRICAN POLITICS Ian Taylor
AFRICAN RELIGIONS
    Jacob K. Olupona
AGEING Nancy A. Pachana
AGNOSTICISM Robin Le Poidevin
AGRICULTURE Paul Brassley and
    Richard Soffe
ALEXANDER THE GREAT
    Hugh Bowden
ALGEBRA Peter M. Higgins
AMERICAN BUSINESS HISTORY
    Walter A. Friedman
AMERICAN CULTURAL HISTORY
    Eric Avila
AMERICAN FOREIGN RELATIONS
    Andrew Preston
AMERICAN HISTORY
    Paul S. Boyer

AMERICAN IMMIGRATION
    David A. Gerber
AMERICAN INTELLECTUAL
    HISTORY
    Jennifer Ratner-Rosenhagen
THE AMERICAN JUDICIAL
    SYSTEM Charles L. Zelden
AMERICAN LEGAL HISTORY
    G. Edward White
AMERICAN MILITARY HISTORY
    Joseph T. Glatthaar
AMERICAN NAVAL HISTORY
    Craig L. Symonds
AMERICAN POETRY David Caplan
AMERICAN POLITICAL HISTORY
    Donald Critchlow
AMERICAN POLITICAL PARTIES
    AND ELECTIONS L. Sandy Maisel
AMERICAN POLITICS
    Richard M. Valelly
THE AMERICAN PRESIDENCY
    Charles O. Jones
THE AMERICAN REVOLUTION
    Robert J. Allison
AMERICAN SLAVERY
    Heather Andrea Williams
THE AMERICAN SOUTH
    Charles Reagan Wilson
THE AMERICAN WEST Stephen Aron
AMERICAN WOMEN'S HISTORY
    Susan Ware
AMPHIBIANS T. S. Kemp
ANAESTHESIA Aidan O'Donnell
ANALYTIC PHILOSOPHY
    Michael Beaney

Available soon:

For more information visit our website

www.oup.com/vsi/

Alan Barenberg

THE GULAG

A Very Short Introduction

OXFORD
UNIVERSITY PRESS

OXFORD
UNIVERSITY PRESS

Oxford University Press is a department of the University of Oxford.
It furthers the University's objective of excellence in research, scholarship,
and education by publishing worldwide. Oxford is a registered trade mark of
Oxford University Press in the UK and in certain other countries.

Published in the United States of America by Oxford University Press
198 Madison Avenue, New York, NY 10016, United States of America.

CIP data is on file at the Library of Congress.

ISBN 978-0-19-754822-6

Integrated Books International, United States of America

Contents

List of illustrations

Acknowledgments

This book draws on the research of too many scholars to name: many of their works can be found in the references and suggestions for further reading. I wish to acknowledge the generosity of Marc Elie who shared research, advice, and the included map. Many of the ideas in this book were developed while completing an edited volume, *Rethinking the Gulag: Identities, Sources, Legacies* (2022), and I wish to thank my collaborators on that project, particularly my co-editor, Emily D. Johnson.

I could not ask for a better scholarly home than the Department of History at Texas Tech University—it is a special place thanks to remarkable colleagues, staff, and students. Research and writing of this book were generously supported by the Buena Vista Foundation, as well as the Office of the Provost, the College of Arts and Sciences, and the Humanities Center (all of Texas Tech University).

I am grateful to the anonymous readers, who provided invaluable feedback. I also wish to thank the staff at Oxford University Press for helping this project see the light of day—especially Nancy Toff, who convinced me to take it on in the first place.

The bulk of the work on this book was completed during the height of the COVID-19 pandemic, circumstances that made me particularly thankful for the love and support of friends and family. Above all, I wish to thank Abby Swingen and Ruby Barenberg, without whom this book (and so much else in life) would not have been possible.

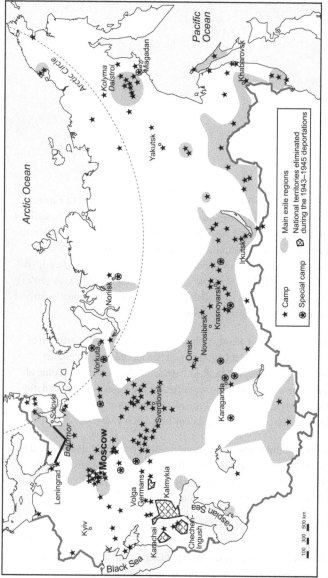

1. A map of the Gulag in 1953, including the main areas of exile and location of camps. It also includes the territories from which entire national groups were exiled during World War II.

Pacific Ocean

Arctic Ocean

Arctic Circle

Kolyma
Dalstroj
⊗ Magadan

Khabarovsk

Yakutsk

Norilsk ⊗

Irkutsk

Vorkuta ⊗

Omsk
Novosibirsk
Krasnoyarsk ⊗

Sverdlovsk

Karaganda ⊗

Solovki

Belomor

Leningrad

Moscow

Kyiv

Volga
Germans

Kalmykia

Karachai

Chechen-
Ingush

Caspian Sea

Black Sea

★ Camp
⊗ Special camp

Main exile regions

National territories eliminated
during the 1943–1945 deportations

100 300 500 km

Chapter 1
What was the Gulag?

Between 1930 and 1960, more than 25 million people were imprisoned or exiled in the Soviet Union. They were held in the Gulag, one of the largest, longest-lasting, and deadliest systems of incarceration and exile in modern history. At its height, it included thousands of prisons, camps, and exile settlements spread across the length and breadth of the Soviet empire. In these institutions, millions toiled to serve the needs of the Soviet economy and to participate, in theory, in the process of their "reforging" (*perekovka*) into full-fledged Soviet citizens. The Gulag was the monstrous product of a system of terror that constantly produced new "enemies" to the social, political, and economic order of Stalinism. The targets of terror shifted constantly, and the Gulag's victims came from a broad cross-section of the population of the Soviet empire. Millions did not survive this carceral system, and those who did survive suffered physical and psychological traumas that would haunt them for the rest of their lives.

The term Gulag entered broad circulation inside and outside the USSR after the publication in 1973 of the first comprehensive study of the Soviet system of incarceration and exile, Aleksandr Solzhenitsyn's *Gulag Archipelago*. A dry term with monstrous significance, "Gulag" is the acronym for an agency created in 1930, the "Main Administration of Camps." Initially overseeing the "corrective labor camps" throughout the USSR, within a few years it controlled a consolidated and centralized system of prisons, camps, and exile settlements. Closely watched by Soviet dictator Iosif Vissarionovich Stalin, it was under the control of the Soviet secret police, successively known as the OGPU, NKVD, and MVD. After a period of reform following Stalin's death in 1953, the Gulag was officially abolished in 1960. Thereafter, control of the Soviet Union's reformed, and much smaller, penal system was devolved to the individual republics. The Gulag's many legacies, however, long outlasted Stalin's lifetime—even today, the penal systems of Russia and other former Soviet republics are strongly shaped by practices established in the 1930s.

The very nature of the Gulag confounds efforts to provide a clear and concise definition. Although many key aspects of the system were established in the early 1930s, it expanded and evolved over time. Its geographic spread was enormous, stretching from the Arctic in the north to the Central Asian steppe in the south, and from the westernmost points in the Soviet empire east to the Pacific. Although it is most closely associated with the labor camp, it included a variety of penal institutions. Often considered to be a tool of political repression, designed to isolate and punish alleged enemies of the Soviet state, the Gulag held prisoners convicted of a wide range of crimes and exiles punished for belonging to a particular class or national category. Prisoners convicted of "ordinary" crimes far outnumbered those convicted of "political" ones, usually by a wide margin. The Gulag also served multiple functions for the Soviet state, including punishment, isolation, social engineering and rehabilitation, and economic exploitation. It was a hybrid system that resists a simple, overarching interpretation.

The Gulag was a linchpin of Stalin's authoritarian system of rule. A decade after the Bolsheviks came to power in the Revolutions of 1917, Stalin launched an all-out effort to transform the USSR into a highly centralized state that could prepare for an inevitable war with the capitalist world. The state outlawed private businesses and sought to manage the entire economy through a system of centralized planning. Stalin ordered his deputies to focus this new economy almost exclusively on the rapid development of heavy industry. A violent campaign crushed the Soviet peasantry, which had been operating as independent farmers since the Bolshevik seizure of power, forcing millions of peasants into state-managed collective farms. Former members of Tsarist elites who had continued to serve important roles in government, industry, and culture were persecuted and removed in favor of a new generation of loyal functionaries. Censorship and crackdowns shattered a relatively open and vibrant cultural landscape, forcing artists to adhere to the narrow and arbitrary standards of the new ruling elite. As they transformed the USSR, Stalin and his advisors sent millions of people to the Gulag. At the same time, the Gulag became one of Stalin's most trusted tools to mold the Soviet Union's political, economic, social, and cultural system.

The functions of the Gulag

The Gulag was a system that combined the goals of punishment and exploitation. It was, first and foremost, a place of punishment for those who transgressed against Soviet state or society, either by their alleged actions or because of how the state classified them by class or national identity. Camps and exile settlements were tools of punishment and retribution against those whom the state deemed to be the most dangerous and untrustworthy. As the Gulag's most famous prisoner and chronicler Aleksandr Solzhenitysn wrote of these penal institutions, "they were invented for *destruction*." Punishment came through forced labor, rules and regulations that treated the inmate population with harshness and violence, and separation from family and familiar surroundings. Isolation from society at large was intended to protect society from active or potential threats, but it also enhanced the degree of punishment that prisoners and exiles faced. Many camps and exile settlements were established far from major population centers, and prisoners and exiles were typically held in locations that were

3

far away from loved ones, a form of "in exile imprisonment" that deprived prisoners of access to their families.

The Gulag also served as a system of mass exploitation of prisoners and exiles. Rather than simply punish and isolate, camps and exile settlements used inmate labor to further the ambitious economic goals of the Stalinist state. Labor was a nearly universal requirement for Gulag inmates, excluding only those held in prisons or those who were completely incapacitated by illness or disability. Work filled most of their waking hours, and days off were extraordinarily rare. The camps used an elaborate system to measure work output, and the fulfillment of production quotas determined the size of prisoners' rations. Labor itself was often the most destructive aspect of life for prisoners and exiles, as they toiled away in jobs that were not only dangerous, but also contributed to chronic hunger, since rations were rarely sufficient to match the effort expended. Avoiding hard labor, whether through dissimulation or being transferred to less physically onerous jobs, was one of the most important strategies that prisoners deployed to increase their chances of survival.

The overwhelming focus on exploitation and punishment largely explain the high rates of illness and death among the Gulag population. Brutal exploitation, deliberate cruelty, and systemic violence permeated the system, and prisoners and exiles died in a variety of circumstances: in a packed cattle car on the way to a place of exile, deprived of food, water, and medical treatment; as punishment for a violation of the camp rules; shot by a guard for an alleged escape; murdered by a fellow prisoner or exile; in an accident at an unsafe workplace; of hypothermia or exposure; of an infectious disease like typhus; of a variety of illnesses associated with lack of nutrition, such as scurvy, or as a result of outright starvation. At least 3.7 million deaths were officially recorded from 1929 to 1953, but the actual number of deaths was significantly higher. Although research at determining mortality is ongoing, it appears that about one in five prisoners and exiles perished from 1930 to 1960. Those who survived endured significant physical and psychological traumas, and many were permanently disabled after release. Thus, the Gulag was also a system of mass death and disability.

The Gulag was seen by Soviet leaders as a tool for the transformation of individuals and social groups. Whereas many modern prison systems focus on the idea that inmates can and should be rehabilitated while incarcerated, the Gulag approached this issue with particular vigor and also with a distinctly Stalinist bent. Camps were intended as places for the active "reforging" of prisoners—and in the early 1930s, during a brief era when Gulag activities were actively publicized, this idea was put front and center. "Reforging" was to be done through a series of activities that would raise the cultural level and political literacy of prisoners. Thus, Soviet leaders conceived of the Gulag as a place where those who had failed to become the "new Soviet person" would receive the opportunity to change course and become successfully reintegrated into Soviet society. Such opportunities to be "re-forged" were not evenly distributed throughout the Gulag population, however—the greater the danger an individual was seen to represent, the more punishment was emphasized over rehabilitation. Yet aside from the most dangerous criminals sentenced to death or "hard labor," Gulag inmates were offered a cultural program aimed at self-improvement and the opportunity to prove themselves through labor. The degree of enthusiasm with which "reforging" was practiced varied greatly both among penal institutions and over time, but the persistence of this idea throughout the Stalin era cannot be ignored.

The Gulag was also a tool for the transformation of the Soviet environment and space. Exile had been used to aid colonization in Imperial Russia, and the Gulag followed this precedent, albeit on a much grander scale. Just as they believed that the Gulag was a tool of social engineering that could transform human nature, Soviet officials believed that forced labor could help the state transform space, triumph over nature, and achieve long-held goals of developing inhospitable regions in the Far North, Siberia, and Central Asia. The rapid industrialization launched under the first five-year plan (1928–32) set extremely ambitious goals at the same time that it unleashed unprecedented chaos in the city and countryside, with huge population movements and rapid labor turnover. In this context, unfree labor seemed to offer an ideal solution—while ridding Soviet society of its most unreliable elements, the state could marshal the organized labor power of prisoners and exiles without concerns about promising wages or living conditions necessary to attract and retain workers. A series of apparent successes, including the construction of the White Sea-Baltic Canal (1932–33), suggested that the Gulag could be used as an effective tool for the state to accomplish its most ambitious goals, particularly in remote and forbidding environments. Both exile settlements and camp complexes were treated as tools for the "colonization" of sparsely populated regions with valuable resources. Like many colonial projects, it was extremely violent, and concern for the colonizers and the colonized rarely figured into the state's grand designs. As they disrupted the natural environment and built new urban landscapes, many Gulag projects were extremely harmful to indigenous populations.

The Gulag was meant to secure Soviet society from those considered to be its enemies. Arrest and deportation were intended to isolate individuals or groups deemed dangerous to the Soviet state and its interests. The Stalinist state policed society increasingly harshly over the course of the 1930s and 1940s; moreover, it tended to view violations of the social order as existential threats. Thus, the list of the Soviet state's enemies constantly expanded over the course of the Stalin era. It included both individuals convicted of specific crimes and entire population categories. The Soviet leadership declared social classes, and later, national groups, to be dangerous to the state, and millions of Soviet citizens were repressed based on how state actors classified their social or national identity. One of the Gulag's most important roles in the Stalinist polity was to protect society from alleged enemies bent on destroying the Soviet Union.

Finally, the Gulag was also a system of mass incarceration or mass imprisonment. While such terms are usually used to refer to the rapid expansion of the prison system in the United States after World War II and its disproportionate effects on racial minorities, they also provide a useful way to think about the Gulag. According to legal scholar David Garland, mass imprisonment includes two conditions: first, a "rate of imprisonment and a size of prison population that is markedly above the historical and comparative norm for societies of this type"; and second, the "concentration of imprisonment's effects" on one or more sections of the population. This definition is largely applicable to the Gulag. The Stalinist USSR clearly incarcerated its population at a very high rate: in 1950, there were more than 1,500 prisoners per 100,000 Soviet citizens—this was more than double the highest rate of incarceration in Russia and the USSR before or after Stalin's rule. Such a rate includes only prisoners—if exiles were included, it would be nearly double. This is perhaps the highest rate of incarceration of any society in the twentieth and twenty-first centuries—by comparison, the highest rate of incarceration in the United States to date is 755 per 100,000 in 2008.

The Gulag also concentrated the effects of incarceration on certain parts of Soviet society. This is most clearly seen in the case of exile operations, which sought to punish and isolate entire social groups on the basis of class, nationality, or a combination of the two. While the camps held a somewhat broader cross-section of the Soviet population, certain social groups, especially the urban underclass, were much more likely to be incarcerated. Thus, it is useful to consider the Gulag to be a system of mass incarceration, as that term captures both the extraordinarily high rate of incarceration and the degree to which the weight of repression fell disproportionately on certain social groups.

The institutions of the Gulag

The institutions of the Gulag were profoundly influenced by the theory and practice of the modern penitentiary. In Foucault's discussion, the modern prison was part of a transformation in how states managed populations—less through physical punishment, as had been the case in the pre-modern era, than through detailed and rational plans to control spaces, bodies, and behaviors. According to Foucault, the modern penitentiary represented an attempt to realize Jeremy Bentham's project of the "panopticon," a building where a single guard could view each prisoner. Such ambitious and utopian visions of disciplining prisoners and exiles were at the core of how Soviet officials saw the Gulag, as the mountains of plans and documents that fill Soviet archives can attest. Yet the majority of Gulag inmates were held in camps or exile settlements, institutions that could not accommodate the impulse to constantly monitor and surveil. Instead, what developed was more of a "polyopticon," where communal life and work meant constant supervision by other inmates, "the many watching the many." Thus, violence between prisoners and networks of informants played key roles in realizing the Soviet vision of the Gulag as a place where inmates could be classified, exploited, and transformed by the state. Although the Gulag is most closely associated with the prison camp, it included a variety of penal institutions.

The Gulag operated a network of prisons across the territory of the USSR. Prisons served two primary functions: first, to hold those suspects or convicts at any stage in the judicial process before beginning a period of punishment in a camp or colony; second, as the location of punishment for those whose alleged crimes warranted the most serious penalty short of execution. Prisoners being held before formal charge or during the process of investigation and trial often faced a grim existence, with overcrowded cells, violence from other prisoners, and various forms of physical and mental torture from investigators. Investigative prisons were at their absolute worst during the period of the so-called Great Terror (August 1937–November 1938), when arrests reached their highest rate in the Stalin era. This created massive overcrowding, and many prisoners recall cells that were so packed that they could only lie down in shifts. This was a period when physical torture was sanctioned as part of the "investigation" process, meaning that many prisoners faced beatings, sleep deprivation, and other forms of violence during long nights in the offices of NKVD investigators. The length of stay in an investigative prison varied widely, from days to months, and much depended upon how quickly a suspect's case reached its conclusion. Although the investigative and judicial process lacked any semblance of a notion of due process, there was nevertheless an emphasis on assembling evidence and a confession, and some cases dragged on for months.

Other prisons, set aside for the punishment of the state's most dangerous criminals, focused on isolation. In such institutions, which were often established in former monasteries, prisoners were typically held in individual cells. Because isolation was emphasized, these prisoners were not required to work, rendering them some of the only inmates in the Gulag whose punishment did not require labor. To heighten punishment and lessen the opportunities for interaction, prisoners rarely spent time outside their cells. Notably, these prisons were the only spaces in the Gulag where prisoners did not live communally. Instead of relying on mutual surveillance and internal policing, these prisons relied on isolation and nearly constant surveillance of prisoners by guards to keep order—thus, they were the only Gulag institutions operated on the model of the "panopticon" rather than the "polyopticon."

Once sentenced, the majority of prisoners served their time in a "corrective labor camp" (ITL) or "corrective labor colony" (ITK). Both terms were, more or less, euphemisms for "concentration camp," a term that was used to refer to Soviet penal camps in the 1920s but fell out of favor at the end of the decade. Camps and colonies varied greatly in size and capacity, holding prisoner populations ranging from the hundreds to over 100,000. Each was organized into subdivisions known as sections (*otdeleniia*) and points (*punkty*), which in turn included one or more self-contained "zones" of detention for prisoners. The larger complexes contained many of these sections and points, often covering hundreds of miles. The largest complex, by far, was the massive Sevvostlag (Northeastern) camp complex in Kolyma, Siberia, which stretched along a 1,200-mile road from Magadan on the Sea of Okhotsk into the Siberian interior. Although each institution was generally organized around a particular economic activity, many of the larger camps and colonies were economically diverse, with prisoners engaged in mining, construction, and agricultural activities.

Camps and colonies were laid out in a manner that was typical for concentration camps, a form of incarceration that originated in European overseas colonies at the turn of the twentieth century but became increasingly common across North America, Europe, and Asia in the 1930s and 1940s. The typical camp subdivision, or "zone," was laid out in a rectangle, surrounded by walls or fences topped in barbed wire, and guarded by men posted in watchtowers. In theory, each zone contained everything that the prisoners needed on a day-to-day basis: living barracks, various administrative offices, warehouses (including a place for prisoners to receive mail and packages), a bakery, kitchen, mess hall, and a bathhouse. Life in the camps was generally focused around work, with prisoners living and working in small brigades. Although some prisoners worked within the zone, typically they worked on a job site outside the camp gates. Thus, a significant part of most prisoners' days was spent outside the camp, either in transit or at work, usually under armed guard.

Although similar in their general structure, camps and colonies occupied different places in the hierarchy of Gulag institutions.

Camps were the priority institution. They were typically assigned the most important tasks in the Gulag's economic portfolio and were also better staffed and better supplied. In general, camps received the prisoners who were healthiest and had the longest sentences, thus representing the largest productive potential. Colonies, on the other hand, were set aside for prisoners with shorter sentences and who were less able to perform hard labor. Thus, they tended to hold a higher percentage of those convicted of ordinary crimes (*bytoviki*) rather than either violent criminals or "politicals." During World War II and the postwar era, prisoner health became the key criterion deciding whether prisoners were held in a camp or colony. As a large proportion of prisoners suffered from hunger or disability, tens of thousands of weak or seriously ill prisoners were transferred from camps to colonies. Though the latter were theoretically better suited allowing for the "convalescence" of ill prisoners, since they had laxer work requirements and were often located in milder climates, in practice they were frequently used as dumping grounds for prisoners from camps who were too weak to work or to recover. Thus, mortality rates were often considerably higher in colonies than they were in camps.

The daily regime, and its harshness, varied greatly between camps and colonies, and often within each complex. The harshest regime camp sections were those set aside after 1943 for *katorga*, or hard labor convicts. Such sections contained enhanced security measures to isolate, punish, and control the movement of the convicts held within. For example, such convicts were required to wear numbers on their uniforms and live in barracks that were locked overnight. This enhanced security regime was extended in 1948 to a much larger group of "special" camps. Other camp sections, set aside for the least dangerous prisoners, enforced a relatively lenient set of regulations. Yet the harshness of camp life varied within individual camp sections, depending on a prisoner's job and place in the camp hierarchy. Both formal hierarchies and informal practices profoundly affected the treatment of prisoners in the camps and colonies.

Soviet camps are frequently compared to their counterparts in Nazi Germany. Both shared the same basic model of the camp—a heavily guarded interior zone encircled by barbed wire or some other physical barrier, separated as much as possible from the surrounding space. Within the boundaries of the camp, all regular rules and legality were suspended, creating what philosopher Giorgio Agamben called the "state of exception." There were, however, significant differences between Gulag camps and Nazi camps. Most prisoners in Nazi camps were not formally charged with crimes and were instead imprisoned indefinitely based on their perceived racial category. Gulag camps and colonies held individuals convicted of specific crimes and given discrete sentences (though most exiles, who were not held within camps, were given an open-ended term of exile based on their class and/or national category). A significant proportion of prisoners in Gulag camps were released every year, whereas release from a Nazi camp was extremely rare. The Gulag's emphasis on "reforging," or rehabilitation, was also very different from the Nazi case, where prisoners were explicitly worked to death. Most importantly, some Nazi camps operated as sites of mass extermination, where prisoners were periodically "selected" for mass murder. While mortality was significant in the Gulag, there was no clear equivalent to the Nazi policy of systematic extermination of certain groups of inmates.

Millions of those punished in the Gulag were not held in camps or prisons. Instead of being formally convicted of crimes, they were instead exiled to so-called "special settlements" in the Soviet Union's peripheries in the north, Siberia, or Central Asia on the basis of their class or national status. These exile villages were the most diverse of the Gulag's institutions—and they also diverged the most from typical modern penal institutions. The "special settlements" were highly regimented, with strict regulations intended to create a reconstituted and highly ordered version of the Soviet peasant village. Labor was mandatory, and exiles who violated the existing order were subject to fines or short-term imprisonment. Villages were administered by officials in the district *komendatura*, with a commandant in each village who was responsible for all matters of administration and answerable to district and regional bosses. The exiles were required to check in with the commandant regularly and were not allowed to leave the villages without official permission.

Exile settlements differed from camps in many important respects. Exiles generally lived as family units in their own dwellings. There were many children in the special settlements: for example, approximately half the population of the "punished peoples" exiled during World War II were under the age of sixteen. Such children were required to attend school, either at one specifically established for exiles in the special settlements, or more often, in existing schools alongside the children of nonexiles. "Special settlements" were far more permeable than camps—they were not physically enclosed spaces with guards. While in theory exile spaces were strictly delimited from those for the "free" population, some villages contained a mixture of exile and non-exile populations. Exiles often lived, worked, and studied alongside those who had been there before they arrived. Intermarriage with nonexiles was not forbidden, and thus "mixed" families abounded. The requirement to check in with the commandant periodically, as well as the threat of harsh criminal punishment, did little to discourage flight. Hundreds of thousands of exiles fled from their "special settlements" in search of a better life elsewhere.

Work was mandatory in the "special settlements." For some exiles, this meant agricultural labor on collective or state farms. Many others, especially adult males, were required to work in industrial enterprises, often at a great distance from their families. Unlike prisoners, "special settlers" received compensation for their work, whether in the form of wages or a share of collective farm output, albeit with a portion deducted for "upkeep." Thus, "special settlers" were not fed according to their output as prisoners were, which made their survival far less precarious once they were established in their places of exile. However, in those cases when exiles had to rely on rations from the Gulag, such as during transportation or after just having arrived at their places of exile, they often faced significant and deadly shortages. Death rates for exiles were thus highest during transportation and in the first years living in exile.

Not all of those convicted of crimes in the Stalinist Soviet Union served time in penal institutions. In addition to the millions held in the Gulag, millions of other convicts were given noncustodial sentences. Such punishments were typically for minor violations of labor discipline like lateness, illegal job-changing, or absenteeism, which were criminalized throughout much of the Stalin era. For example, according to a June 1940 labor decree any worker whose lateness resulted in more than twenty minutes of lost work time could be sentenced to six months' work at a reduced wage. "Corrective labor" outside the Gulag was much less harsh than it was for those held in camps and other Gulag institutions, and it involved neither separation from one's family nor relocation to a remote area. Nevertheless, it made day-to-day life much more difficult for those convicted.

Additionally, millions who were never formally convicted of a crime were nevertheless imprisoned in Gulag camps. Particularly during World War II and the postwar era, several different groups of people were held in camps despite not being considered prisoners in a formal sense. This included "refugees" from the Soviet Union's western borderlands, Soviet soldiers who had been freed from German POW camps, Soviet civilians suspected of having collaborated with enemy occupiers during the war, and Soviet Germans who had been exiled but who were subsequently "mobilized" to work in Gulag camps to support the war effort. The largest of these groups consisted of foreign POWs, over 2 million of whom were held in a separate system of camps from 1943 through 1949. Regulations for holding these populations were generally modeled after those used for prisoners in regular Gulag camps. Labor was mandatory, living conditions were often brutal, and these nonprisoners faced many of the same risks to their health and life as did those who were technically prisoners.

The Gulag, state, and society

On paper, the Soviet Gulag appears to have been a highly centralized and bureaucratic institution, governed by a strict set of clearly defined regulations. However, archival sources and survivor testimony demonstrate that the appearance of order is often misleading. In fact, as was typical for Soviet institutions in the Stalin era, a peek behind the façade of "totalitarian" control suggests that it was a system beset by bureaucratic conflict, arbitrariness, and chronic shortages. Margarete Buber-Neumann, a German communist who was imprisoned in both a Soviet camp (Karlag, in Kazakhstan) and a German camp (Ravensbrück), remarks in her memoirs on the striking difference between the chaos of Soviet camps and the orderliness of their German counterparts. What she experienced in a Soviet camp was starkly different from the "Prussian thoroughness" and "pedantic nightmare" of the German camp. The Gulag was constantly short of food, clothing, and other supplies for inmates, particularly during times of crisis such as the famine of 1932–33 and World War II. Thus, the amount and quality of food that prisoners received in their rations was typically below what was required by regulations, significantly lowering their chances of survival. Personnel shortages were exacerbated by the enormous size and spread of penal institutions across the territory of the Soviet Union.

Given long distances and poor transportation and communications infrastructure, central authorities had little choice but to delegate enormous responsibilities and authority to camp bosses and "special settlement" commandants—authority that was often then delegated to the bosses of smaller subunits. This led, not surprisingly, to corruption and arbitrariness at all levels of the Gulag administration. While central authorities exercised periodic oversight of the camps and "special settlements," local administrators were generally granted great latitude on matters both routine and extraordinary. This was especially true in the case of exile settlements, where a single commandant might be responsible for keeping track of hundreds of families in remote locations with poor transportation and communication links. Daily life in the Gulag was subject to many rules and regulations, but it was also profoundly influenced by chronic shortages and the complex relationship between center and periphery.

Shortages, chaos, and inefficiency meant that the living conditions for inmates were typically worse than what central regulations dictated. Yet such situations also created opportunities for prisoners and exiles to exercise limited agency over their own fates. Trading in goods that were in short supply offered the opportunity for some inmates to improve their odds of survival. Labor shortages meant that thousands of prisoners and exiles were used in unexpected roles, including as guards, supervisors, and engineers—even as this violated Gulag regulations. Such jobs meant temporarily avoiding the dangers of hard labor and often allowed access to camp resources that could be used to a prisoner's benefit. Thus, the nature of the Gulag itself provided opportunities for everyday resistance to a cruel and inhuman system. While inmates did not control their own fates, some had opportunities to exploit the system for the benefit of themselves or others whom they tried to help.

The Gulag was closely connected to Soviet society at large, and these interconnections and interactions profoundly affected daily life for its inmates. Solzhenitsyn used the metaphor of the archipelago to characterize the system of camps and exile settlements, suggesting that carceral institutions were islands separated both from each other and from the mainland of Soviet life. Yet subsequent research demonstrates that the Gulag was not nearly as isolated as Solzhenitsyn's metaphor suggests. Between 20 and 40 percent of prisoners in the Gulag were released every year during the Stalin era. While many of these releases were because prisoners had become chronically ill or disabled, the release rate was substantial, suggesting that prisoners frequently circulated back into Soviet society on the "outside."

In addition, penal institutions were not always strictly isolated from the settlements that surrounded them. Exiles lived in towns and villages where there were no physical barriers to prevent escape, only the legal requirement to check in periodically with the local commandant. In fact, they frequently lived among nonexiles. Not surprisingly, escapes were frequent, and hundreds of thousands of exiles permanently resettled in Soviet cities where they attempted to hide their status. Camps were typically high-security institutions, surrounded by physical barriers and guarded by men with automatic rifles. Yet shortages of barbed wire and building materials meant that many remote camps were not physically closed off from their surroundings for years after they were established. Further, prisoners typically worked outside the boundaries of the camps, providing them with regular opportunities to interact with nonprisoners outside the camp. Thus, the Gulag was not just a fundamental part of the Soviet system throughout the Stalin era, its inmates remained an important part of Soviet society.

It is essential to acknowledge the diversity of institutions, inmates, and experiences in the Stalinist Gulag, a system that existed for three decades. Although both prisoners and exiles faced forced labor and a profound loss of liberties, life in camp was very different from life in exile. Additionally, the timing of arrest, exile, and imprisonment had an enormous effect on inmates' treatment and prospects for survival, as did the location to which they were sent. How the state classified each inmate, in terms of criminal charge, sentence, or exile group, also mattered. In some circumstances, death was more likely than survival for inmates—whereas in others, the mortality rate differed little from its level among the Soviet population at large. Each inmate brought into the Gulag their own identity and life trajectory that influenced their experiences. Overall, however, the agency that Gulag inmates could exercise during imprisonment or exile varied greatly, and the factors that most strongly influenced their prospects of survival were typically beyond their control.

Given the complexity of the Gulag and its place in Soviet society and history, it is best understood via examination from a variety of perspectives. By considering the interplay and conflict between central regulations and local practices, the remarkable variety of inmates, penal institutions, and experiences, inmate agency and forms of resistance, and the interconnectedness of penal institutions with life on the "outside," the outlines of this massive system emerge. The Gulag was a product of the Stalinist system, one focused on transforming society into a Utopia and humans into "new Soviet people"—yet it was woefully unable to achieve these goals. Thus, the Gulag's deadliness and profound inhumanity cannot simply be explained by its intended purposes to punish, exploit, transform, and isolate. A significant part of its monstrous potential to destroy human lives came from the irreconcilable gap between Soviet leaders' Utopian visions and the relatively limited capacities of the state that they built.

Chapter 2
The origins and evolution of the Stalinist Gulag

From 1929 until 1953, the Gulag grew from a small system of prisons and camps into one of the largest carceral systems in modern history. Its foundation, growth, and evolution were closely tied to the tremendous changes unleashed by the state upon society from the beginning of Stalin's "revolution from above" in 1929. The aims of this revolution amounted to no less than the total transformation of the Soviet state and society, including both rapid, state-managed industrialization and the violent "collectivization" of agriculture, whereby peasants were forced out of independent agriculture into state-run farms. Although there had been discussion and experimentation in the 1920s, radical changes to the scale and nature of the Soviet penal system did not begin until Stalin launched these twin campaigns of industrialization and collectivization. The Gulag was subsequently shaped by a series of campaigns and crises of the Stalin era, including the Great Terror of 1937–38, World War II, and postwar reconstruction. Although there were brief periods of contraction, the size of the prisoner and exile populations grew dramatically as new categories of the population were designated as enemies and new behaviors were criminalized. Over the course of twenty-five years, the state built penal institutions across the Soviet Union's vast territory, establishing the Gulag as one of the pillars of the Stalinist system. The Gulag was not merely a dumping ground for criminals, perceived political enemies, and members of class or national groups deemed to be dangerous: it was also a key tool in the Stalinist project of transforming society, the economy, and space itself.

Soviet prisons before the Gulag

When the Bolsheviks assumed power in 1917, they were already well acquainted with the intricacies of incarceration, albeit from the perspective of the prisoner rather than the jailer. Like the members of other underground political parties in pre-revolutionary Russia, many of their leaders had been arrested and spent a significant amount of time in prison, Tsarist hard labor (*katorga*), or Siberian exile. When setting policies, they drew upon their experiences as well as Marxist theory, which they had largely learned through the works of Vladimir Lenin, the leader and chief theorist of the Bolsheviks before his death in 1924. They believed that crime was a product of capitalism and would diminish with the decline of class exploitation, eventually disappearing in a communist society. In the meantime, imprisonment would be a tool of rehabilitation rather than retribution. Thus, the Bolsheviks envisioned their system of incarceration to be temporary. While it existed, it would be fundamentally different from that of any nonsocialist society.

However, these notions of radically altering the system of crime and punishment were tempered by the actual experience of governing. The Bolsheviks had to contend with both the system of incarceration that they inherited and the brutal civil war and famine that followed the 1917 Revolution. The Tsarist prison system had experienced both rapid growth and concerted reforms since the late nineteenth century. On the eve of World War I, there were approximately 177,000 people held in the Russian prison system, a number that had increased significantly from the figure of 85,000 in 1900. Of these, 29,300 were held in *katorga* ("hard labor") prisons, and 34,750 in correctional prisons (IAO)—the two penal institutions where labor was obligatory. Exile was perhaps even more common than incarceration as a punishment. In 1898 it was estimated that there were just short of 300,000 exiles in Siberia. Russia's vastness and sparsely populated Siberian hinterland had played an important role in penal policy for centuries, and exiles were expected to aid colonization.

Penal institutions in the early Soviet era were remarkably chaotic and decentralized. Most prisoners were held in existing prisons or in hastily established camps, often located in monasteries or other religious institutions. By the end of 1927, there were approximately 200,000 inmates, a modest increase from the total at the beginning of World War I. Places of confinement were controlled by competing institutions, chiefly the People's Commissariat of Justice (NKIu), People's Commissariat of Internal Affairs (NKVD), and the secret police (known as the ChK, VChK, later the GPU and then OGPU), each of which sought control over more prisoners. It was not until 1934 that a single agency, the USSR NKVD, assumed control of all places of confinement in the USSR, marking a victory for the secret police in the struggle for control of the Soviet Union's system of incarceration.

Although the scale of incarceration did not increase in the first decade after the 1917 Revolution, the Bolsheviks experimented with new penal policies, particularly in the Solovki (SLON) camp complex. This camp complex was established in October 1923 in the Solovetsky Islands archipelago, site of one of the most important Orthodox monasteries in Russia. Many long-term Gulag policies were developed in Solovki. Bucking tradition, prisoners convicted of political offenses were held together with other convicts. In an attempt to increase labor efficiency in agriculture, forestry, and other economic enterprises, prisoners were fed depending on how well they fulfilled their production plan. This system of differentiated rations would later become a fundamental part of life for prisoners in the Gulag. The Solovki complex was also a key testing ground for cultural activities intended to educate and "reforge" prisoners. Absent a significant expansion of repression against the Soviet population, such experiments remained limited, however.

The Gulag and the Stalin Revolution

It was Stalin's revolution from above, and its twin goals of transforming both agriculture and industry across the Soviet Union, that fundamentally altered the scale of repression and provided the impetus for the penal experiments of the 1920s to be implemented on a broad scale. In only a few short years, the Gulag became a vast network of camps and exile settlements and a linchpin of the Stalinist system. By the middle of the 1930s, the Gulag was already a sprawling, centrally controlled system of exile and incarceration that had spread to nearly every corner of the country and every sector of the economy.

The mass exile of peasants to remote villages came first. In the winter of 1929–30, Stalin and the Politburo ordered the wholesale collectivization of agriculture. They admonished Party and state authorities to ensure that Soviet peasants, who had been resistant to state reforms, join the new system of collective farms en masse. The orders to carry out this process were deliberately vague, inviting coercion. They also included instructions to escalate violence and repression in the countryside against alleged "kulaks" (rich peasants). Those falling under this category were to be expropriated and removed from villages via arrest or exile. In all, some 2.2 million "kulaks" were deported in the first half of the 1930s, at least 1.8 million in 1930–31 alone. They were resettled as entire families, including both children and the elderly. Rather than being charged with a specific crime and sentenced for a particular length of time, these "special settlers," as they were officially known, were given what amounted to open-ended terms of exile. These exiles represented a massive pool of unfree laborers that the secret police eagerly put to work in agriculture and forestry in the north, Urals regions, and Siberia.

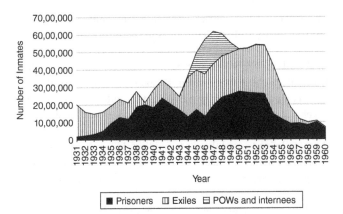

2. A chart showing the total population of prisoners, exiles, POWs, and internees, 1931–60. It includes POWs and internees but does not include those given noncustodial sentences or those who were held in camps without formal charges.

Soviet leaders saw the exile settlement as an ideal penal institution, since they believed it would allow for both financial self-sufficiency and the "colonization" of sparsely populated regions. In fact, in 1930 the secret police leadership expressed the belief that the exile village was much more economically sustainable than the camp, since a small group of officials could effectively supervise thousands of exiles. Yet deportation operations were hastily organized and chaotic, and many exiles became seriously ill or died in transit to villages. Conditions in their places of exile were often catastrophic. Although the secret police developed detailed instructions for how exile villages were to be established and operated, these were only distributed *after* hundreds of thousands had been deported. The regulations also assumed adequate personnel, infrastructure, and supplies, which were in short supply or simply absent. Mass death and mass escapes were common in the first years of "kulak" exile.

The network of exile villages was not the only component of the growing Gulag. In 1929 Stalin and the Politburo decreed that prisoners sentenced to terms of more than three years be put to work building the Soviet economy. They ordered the secret police to establish "concentration camps" (soon renamed "corrective labor camps") following the model that the authorities in Solovki developed in the 1920s. At the same time, there was harsh repression against those deemed to threaten the social order, as Soviet policing treated threats to public order as challenges to the supremacy of the state itself. Campaigns against various "social marginals," from former members of the "exploiting classes" of the bourgeoisie to hooligans and homeless children, continuously filled the prisons and camps of the growing Gulag. A draconian theft law adopted in 1932 resulted in the conviction of thousands to long terms of incarceration for petty theft. In short, the Stalinist state criminalized more behaviors and punished illegal acts in progressively harsher ways, continuously expanding the ranks of prisoners. Whereas there had been less than 90,000 criminal convictions across the USSR in 1927, by 1933 this number had risen to over 630,000. By January 1936, there were nearly 1.3 million prisoners in Gulag places of incarceration.

In 1929–30 the Politburo ordered the establishment of a new network of camp complexes to harness prisoner labor to advance the state's economic goals. The NKVD established various regional camp clusters, including those in the Ukhta region of Komi ASSR and Dal'stroi (the "Far Eastern Construction Trust") in Kolyma in northeastern Siberia, to extract coal, oil, and gold in remote areas. Like the exile settlements, they were also seen as a tool for "colonization" of remote regions. At the same time, the Gulag took on the first of many large infrastructure projects: the White Sea-Baltic Canal (BBK), a waterway that created a shipping route between Leningrad and Arkhangelsk. Completed in 1933, its construction resulted in enormous loss of life, and it was ultimately of limited industrial or strategic use due to its shallowness. Nevertheless, Stalin considered it a success because of how quickly it was completed, and the Gulag played a key role in large infrastructure projects over the following two decades. Thus, in only a few short years the Gulag had emerged in its full-blown form: a vast penal system holding millions of exiles and prisoners in a sprawling network of "special settlements" and "corrective labor camps."

The Gulag and the Great Terror

Stalin created the Gulag as part of his campaigns to remake the USSR's countryside and cities during the first five-year plan, and the Great Terror of 1937–38 further shaped the system's development. Fearing disloyalty among the population and a lack of preparedness for war, Stalin launched a series of overlapping campaigns and police operations intended to protect Soviet state and society from perceived internal and external threats. In addition to launching new campaigns to arrest and punish suspected enemies, his deputies modified judicial procedures to accelerate the generation and processing of criminal cases. The tool of mass exile, which had been applied against the "kulak" class enemies in the early part of the decade, was now turned against national groups suspected of being loyal to foreign enemies, beginning more than a decade of "ethnic cleansing" operations. Applied with extreme pressure from above to meet quotas and targets, the terror ushered in unprecedented chaos and fear throughout the Gulag system.

The pace of arrests had barely slackened after the Stalin Revolution—but it accelerated decisively in 1937–38 as Stalin launched a series of large-scale operations aimed at perceived enemies. The largest of these was so-called "mass operations" that targeted a broad range of "hidden enemies" throughout Soviet society. Launched via order no. 00447 in August 1937, it resulted in 1.5 million new convictions in sixteen months—and at least 680,000 of these victims were sentenced to death. The remainder were sentenced to terms in Gulag camps, leading to massive overcrowding and a dramatic worsening of living conditions. Despite orders to expedite investigations, there was soon a huge backlog of cases, and many prisoners spent months in severely overcrowded conditions. Seeking to speed up the process and uncover more enemies, Stalin approved the use of physical torture. NKVD officers dispensed brutal beatings, sleep deprivation, and other means of physical coercion to secure quick confessions and to push prisoners to implicate others in vast criminal conspiracies. The memoirist Evgeniia Ginzburg was arrested in February 1937 but was not actually transferred to a camp until July 1939, having spent more than two years in various prisons. The conditions in which she was held were so poor that Ginzburg and her comrades were initially relieved to be packed onto a train to be sent off to a camp. As she wrote:

> I had time to notice that my car was Number 7. It was a freight car and we were crowded in so that there was scarcely room to stand. But this cheered us up, in view of the prison rule: the more dirty, crowded, and hungry you are, and the more unpleasant the guards, the more likely you are to stay alive. So far, the rule had proved true, so thank heaven for our cattle-car conditions and the guards' rudeness. Good-by to Stolypin cars [special prison cars for prisoners], solitary confinement cells, punishment cells, and polite Vulturidzes [a derogatory nickname for a prison governor]!

The strain from overcrowding soon spread from prisons to the camps. Supplies of food, clothing, and shelter did not keep pace with the rapid increase in the camp population. Conditions in existing camps became catastrophic—a report sent to Stalin in February 1938 described desperate shortages of food, warm clothing, shoes, and housing. In BAMlag, a large railroad construction camp in Siberia, infectious diseases were rampant, and the shortage of clothing was so severe that authorities could not force some prisoners to work because they had nothing to wear. With existing camps struggling to handle the large volume of new prisoners, Stalin ordered the creation of several new camps, largely in the logging industry, calculating that such camps could be hastily and cheaply established. Conditions in these new logging camps were particularly deadly, especially in the winter of 1937–38. A large percentage prisoners became too ill to work, and in the four-month period from December 1937 through March 1938, there were 12,000 recorded prisoner deaths in these new camps, a figure that represented nearly half of official mortality throughout all Gulag camps.

The imperative to find and punish hidden enemies extended to the camps themselves. Order no. 00447 set an initial quota of 10,000 "hidden enemies" in Gulag camps to be identified and executed. However, the quota was eagerly "overfulfilled" and the final number of victims was significantly higher. In the Ukhtpechlag system (Komi ASSR), for example, camp authorities had little trouble identifying prisoners to meet their execution quota. They began with those who had participated in hunger strikes in 1936, many of whom were former members of the Trotskyist opposition to Stalin—and continuously expanded the web of victims. After their cases were processed, prisoners were gathered at two specific sites in the sprawling complex, and executions were carried out in large groups. In all, just over 2,500 prisoners in Ukhtpechlag were executed from December 1937 through November 1938, nearly 5 percent of the total number of prisoners in the complex. Although sentences were supposed to be carried out in strict secrecy, wild rumors and conspiracy theories circulated throughout the camp region, creating an atmosphere of heightened fear and suspicion.

Although most victims of the Great Terror were ordinary people, the government also targeted state and party officials for arrest. Stalin used the terror as a pretext to weed out ineffective or potentially disloyal officials. In the Gulag, this meant that some perpetrators became victims. Many long-serving camp chiefs were arrested, shot, and replaced, including Eduard Berzin, the powerful chief of the Dalstroi camp and industrial system in Kolyma. The head of the NKVD itself, Nikolai Ezhov, was removed from his position in November 1938, and later arrested and executed. His successor, Lavrentii Beriia, removed many of Yezhov's proteges, replacing them with his own loyalists. Such personnel turnover contributed to chaos and disorganization within the Gulag.

The Gulag's exile system fundamentally changed during the Great Terror. Whereas deportations during collectivization had targeted class enemies, in 1935 Stalin began ordering deportations according to national criteria, that is, the nationality listed on the victim's passport. The first such operations were intended to bolster border security, and they targeted national groups living near borders where there were many co-nationals living across the border, outside the USSR. The first such deportation, which took place in 1935, was the expulsion of Soviet Finns living near Finland in the Leningrad and Karelia regions. In all, more than 23,000 people were deported to Western Siberia, the Urals, and Kazakhstan. Stalin's justification for such deportations was that members of the targeted populations might be more loyal to their foreign co-nationals than to the Soviet state. Other deportations followed the forced resettlement of Soviet Finns, including the largest prewar operation carried out according to national criteria: the deportation of Soviet Koreans from the Soviet Far East. Beginning in August 1937 and lasting four months, the NKVD deported over 172,000 Soviet Koreans to Kazakhstan and Uzbekistan. This was the first clear case of the ethnic cleansing of an entire national group under Stalin. In the next decade, it would be followed by several other deportations intended to isolate and punish entire national groups. By the end of 1938, there were nearly 3 million prisoners and exiles in the Gulag.

The Gulag and World War II

World War II transformed the Soviet Union as a whole, and the Gulag was no exception. Stalin continued to use exile as a tool to isolate and punish suspect national groups, and the system of "special settlements" grew dramatically throughout the war. But the population of the camps declined significantly for the first time since before the Stalin Revolution, owing to a variety of factors: loss of territory to the invading armies, mass releases of prisoners to fight at the front, and most of all, the dramatic deterioration of conditions in the camps themselves, where starvation and related illnesses led to unprecedented rates of mortality and disability. Faced with a huge labor deficit, Stalin ordered the mobilization of new groups to be held in camps and subjected to forced labor. Although these forced laborers were not strictly speaking prisoners, in practice they were held in the same camps and subjected to the same cruel regime. Despite the prisoner population declining by more than 1 million from 1941–43, by 1944–45 the Gulag held more exiles, prisoners, and other forced laborers than it had at any time in the 1930s.

During the war, Stalin dramatically expanded the use of exile as punishment in the Gulag. After the Soviet army invaded Eastern Poland, Latvia, Lithuania, and Estonia in 1939–40 in the wake of the Molotov-Ribbentrop pact (the agreement between Hitler and Stalin to divide the territories in Eastern Europe that separated Germany and the USSR), deportations were used to subdue and "Sovietize" the occupied territories. Such deportations were different from those earlier in the decade—rather than ridding internal territories of potential enemies, these were intended to secure control over newly occupied territories. Notably, both nationality and class were used as criteria in these deportations, which affected over 380,000 Poles, Ukrainians, Jews, Belarusians, Latvians, Lithuanians, and Estonians. It was primarily members of the "bourgeoisie" of these national groups who were targeted, although this was a flexible category that was applied to a wide range of victims. Such deportations were reprised at the end of the war and in the immediate postwar period, as the Soviets reestablished control of these territories and fought against active nationalist insurrections in Western Ukraine and the Baltics. This second round of deportations involved more than 300,000 additional deportees. Many of these exiles were sent to work in the Soviet logging industry.

After the outbreak of war with Germany, Stalin ordered the deportation of entire national groups to Siberia and Central Asia. The first wave of these deportations was the "preventive" deportation of groups suspected of owing greater loyalty to enemy states because of their nationality. Thus, virtually the entire Soviet populations of Germans, Finns, and Greeks were deported in late 1941, putatively out of fear that such people would give aid to the invading armies of Germany and its allies. More than 1 million people were exiled under the auspices of these operations, which largely continued the deportation operations of the Great Terror, albeit on a much broader scale.

"Retributive" deportations that punished entire national groups for alleged collaboration with the Germans and their allies constituted another type of wartime "ethnic cleansing" operations. Altogether, nearly 1 million Soviet citizens belonging to several national groups, including the Balkars, Chechens, Crimean Tatars, Ingush, Kalmyks, Karachai, Kurds, and Meshkhetian Turks, were ethnically cleansed from territories that had been officially recognized as their homelands in the 1920s. After the German occupation of their territories ended, they were violently relocated to Kazakhstan, Uzbekistan, and Siberia. After exile, the official homelands of these "punished peoples" were scrubbed from the map of the Soviet Union. Overall, by the end of the war there were over 2.2 million Soviet citizens living in permanent exile, with most of them being held on the basis of their national origin.

3. This logging brigade consisted of exiles from Lithuania, 1950. This photograph speaks to the importance of national identity and community in the Gulag. Lithuanian exiles, like other exiled national groups, relied on aid from their co-nationals to increase their chances of survival.

State policies, as well as the course of the war, affected Gulag camps differently. After reaching an apex of nearly 2.5 million prisoners in January 1941, the camp population declined dramatically in the first years of war with Germany. Following Operation Barbarossa in June 1941, some camps were evacuated to the east, but many were abandoned in the wake of the enemy advance, reducing the overall prisoner population accordingly. Desperate to bolster the ranks of the Red Army, Stalin ordered the mass conscription of prisoners, many of whom were granted early release so they could be sent to the front. Overall, 1.2 million prisoners were conscripted into the Red Army from July 1941 until May 1945. While some were sent to regular military units, after Stalin's "Not One Step Back" order (no. 227) of July 1942, which introduced harsh punishments for unauthorized retreat or surrender, many were assigned to penal units. The chances of survival in such units were very slim, as they were often sent into battle poorly prepared and armed.

Those prisoners left in the camps, as well as those who were newly convicted of crimes, experienced extraordinarily grim conditions, especially in 1941–43. Wartime shortages and decisions to redirect food, medicine, and other supplies from the camps to the front meant that death rates were much higher than at any other time in the Gulag's existence. It is difficult to measure just how bad conditions were: while official death rates increased substantially, so did practices intended to minimize official mortality. Camp authorities granted early medical release to prisoners with no hope of survival so that their deaths would not be recorded as having occurred in a camp. Those prisoners who did survive the war years often contracted severe illnesses and many were permanently disabled. At a time when the Gulag was mobilized for the wartime economy, it had a workforce that was dramatically diminished in numbers and labor capacity. It was not until 1944 that the prisoner population began to increase once again.

Stalin and his advisors compensated for the catastrophic decline in the number and health of prisoners by expanding the ranks of forced laborers via administrative order. Whereas camps typically held prisoners with specific convictions and sentences, during the war hundreds of thousands of Soviet and foreign citizens were sent to camps without formal charges. The first such group was a subset of those deported from Poland, Western Ukraine, and Belarus after the Soviet occupation in 1939—among the tens of thousands exiled to Soviet territory, some, like the Polish Jew Julius Margolin, were instead sent to Gulag camps without a conviction. The largest group of exiles held in the camps consisted of Soviet Germans who, after having been deported wholesale in 1941, were subsequently "mobilized" from their places of exile to work in camps beginning in 1942. More than 400,000 Soviet Germans were thus sent to camps for the duration of the war. Although they were not technically prisoners and were supposed to be separated from the general camp population, both "refugees" and "mobilized" Germans were subject to the usual Gulag camp security regime and conditions. Additionally, many prisoners whose sentences expired during the war were nevertheless held in the camps until the war's conclusion, representing yet another example of the use of forced laborers in the camps who were not, strictly speaking, serving sentences. According to Gulag records, some 115,000 former prisoners were tied to specific camps and worksites under this policy.

As the Soviet Union regained territory during the war, camps were used as temporary places of confinement for those suspected of collaboration, providing the Gulag with another source of labor during the period of investigation. Soviet soldiers who had been captured by the Germans were exploited in this way. Beginning in December 1941, freed POWs were sent to either new or existing camps while they were investigated for being potential "betrayers of the motherland, spies or saboteurs." Like "mobilized" Germans, they were isolated from ordinary prisoners, but were subjected to virtually the same regime. Some were eventually convicted of war crimes and became prisoners, but most were subsequently exiled. In addition, many Soviet civilians who had lived under enemy occupation during the war were subjected to forced labor while their wartime activities were investigated. In May 1945 there were more than 160,000 Soviet citizens in this situation, the majority of whom were put to work in coal mines. Thus, although the prisoner population declined throughout much of the war, several hundred thousand forced laborers of other kinds were held in the camps. Combined with the significant increase in the use of exile during the war, this meant that the population of prisoners, exiles, and other confined populations was over 4 million at the beginning of 1945, twice what it had been at the beginning of 1939.

The Gulag after the war

Following the Soviet declaration of victory in May 1945, Stalin announced an amnesty that freed or lowered the sentences of many categories of Gulag prisoners. It was the first and only such broad amnesty issued during his lifetime. As a result, over 600,000 prisoners were released in the next several months, representing nearly 40 percent of the Gulag prisoner population. While meant as a symbol of Soviet victory and Stalin's generosity, it did not represent a fundamental change in Gulag policy. Largely intended to release prisoners who were too ill or emaciated to work productively for the state, it excluded many categories of prisoners, and it did not apply to exiles at all. Ultimately, it did not lead to a long-term decline in the Gulag population. The population of the Gulag increased and reached its peak in the postwar era. Between 1946 and 1953, between 5 and 6 million prisoners, exiles, and foreign POWs were held in the system.

During and after the war, the Gulag relied heavily on a new source of unfree labor: captured POWs from Axis armies. Beginning with the victory at Stalingrad in 1943, thousands of enemy combatants were sent into the interior of the Soviet Union for forced labor. Most were German, although the captured POWs included Japanese, Romanians, Italians, Austrians, Hungarians, and Finns. The widespread use of POW forced labor began in 1944, and by the beginning of 1945 there were nearly 1 million in Soviet camps. They were held in a separate system known as the GUPVI (Main Administration for the Affairs of POWs and the Interned) that had been established for the labor exploitation of POWs. Yet the connections between the Gulag and the GUPVI were obvious, especially since the latter was also run by the NKVD/MVD, and the camps were run according to the same model that had been established in the Gulag proper. At the beginning of 1946 the number of POWs reached an apex of approximately 2 million. The population of foreign POWs in the camps declined thereafter—in addition to high death rates, POWs were systematically repatriated. The GUPVI was permanently closed in 1950, marking a formal end to Soviet exploitation of foreign POWs. However, a small number of POWs were convicted of war crimes and held in regular Gulag camps—and such prisoners would not be amnestied and released from the Gulag until 1955. Although GUPVI camps existed in every Soviet republic except Tajikistan, most POWs were used to rebuild infrastructure destroyed during the war.

When it came to its domestic population, Soviet penal policy became even more repressive after the war, and the prisoner population increased accordingly. Police operations against nationalist groups in the western borderlands after the war led to an influx of tens of thousands of prisoners from Western Ukraine, Latvia, Lithuania, and Estonia. Even more significant in terms of overall numbers were new antitheft laws adopted in 1947. From 1946 to 1949, nearly 1.4 million Soviet citizens were convicted of theft, and by the beginning of 1953 more than 1.2 million Gulag inmates had theft convictions, representing over half of the total prisoner population. Continuing trends that began during the war, when sentences of 15 to 20 years were meted out to "hard labor" (*katorga*) convicts for certain crimes, sentences ranging from

10 to 25 years became far more common, resulting in a longer average sentence length for prisoners. In January 1948 just over 5 percent of prisoners had sentences of greater than 10 years. By 1951 the share had risen to nearly one-quarter, and by 1953 it had increased to 30 percent. Thus, the size of the camp population increased both because of increased arrests and because prisoners typically served longer sentences.

As the camp system expanded, there were significant efforts to reorganize the prisoner population. Following mass starvation during the war, authorities sought to sort the population by health status so that stronger prisoners would labor in higher priority camps and weaker prisoners would be given the opportunity to recover (while still working) in so-called "convalescence" camps. Although the camp authorities claimed some successes in improving the overall health of the prisoner population after the war, such assertions must be treated with skepticism. While official and unofficial death rates certainly decreased after the war (outside of the famine year of 1947–48), this is only in contrast to the wartime era of extreme deprivation and mass death in the camps.

The postwar era also saw attempts to sort prisoners more finely based on their perceived danger to the state. In 1948 Stalin and Beriia ordered the creation of "special" camps for particularly dangerous prisoners, a network that eventually held more than 250,000 prisoners in twelve camps. The regime in these camps was especially harsh, as prisoners were referred to only by numbers, which they wore on their uniforms, and were used only in the heaviest physical labor. As former prisoner Georgii Demidov described in his short story, "No Toe Tag," the goal of the harsh conditions was to increase the hopelessness of the prisoners held within. Imagining the reactions of the men sent to build barracks in one of the new special camps, he wrote:

> The barracks at Dumb-Luck Creek were built according to the same standard principles [of low quality]. But here's what was baffling to

the builders: they were ordered to build stout grates into the dim windows and hang heavy barn locks on the outsides of the doors. It might have been funny—you could have broken through the wall anywhere you liked with the help of an ordinary stake or poker—if people didn't understand that the reason for the grating and locks had nothing to do with securing the barracks. Without a doubt, their significance lay in their oppressive effect on the barracks' future inhabitants.

Any "especially dangerous" prisoners released at the end of their sentences were ordered to remain in perpetual exile in remote regions of Siberia and the North. Yet for most prisoners, conditions in the postwar Gulag generally improved, especially when compared with the bleak conditions of the war and the postwar famine of 1947–48. Food and medical care improved, and there were concerted efforts to incentivize labor by introducing a system of wages for prisoners.

The size of the USSR's exile population continued to grow after the war, albeit at a much slower pace. Between the end of the war and Stalin's death, nearly 400,000 people were sent into exile, most of whom were deported from the Soviet Union's western borderlands as Soviet rule was reestablished in Western Ukraine, the Baltics, and Moldova. This furthered the transformation of exile from an institution that targeted victims based on class identity to one that was primarily used to punish people based on their national identity—as of 1948, only about 150,000 "kulaks" remained in exile, which was approximately 6 percent of the total population.

As was the case with the Gulag "special" camps, Stalin sought to make the regime in postwar "special settlements" even harsher and more heavily regulated than had been the case during the war. Gulag administrators constantly fretted about the lack of personnel and order in the special settlements, with thousands of exiles fleeing or otherwise missing from population counts. As of

4. Born in Moscow in 1931, Iurii Valentinovich Ivanov-Naidenov was arrested and convicted in 1951 for "participation in an anti-Soviet group and anti-Soviet agitation." Shown here in his prison uniform and wearing his number, EE-666, he was a prisoner in a special camp in Kazakhstan. Special camp prisoners like Ivanov-Naidenov were identified by numbers rather than names as part of a concerted effort to dehumanize and punish certain groups of convicts beyond what was required by the regime for ordinary prisoners.

January 1, 1948, there were 17,000 suspected escapees from the special settlements. In order to stem the tide of escapes, in November 1948 the state took the extraordinary measure of making the punishment for escape twenty years of "hard labor," ensuring both long sentences and the harshest conditions for those caught. Thousands were convicted of this harsh punishment, although there is little evidence that escapes from exile settlements abated as a result. Overall, the exile system grew larger than it had been at any other point in the Stalin era, and total number of exiles reached an apex of over 2.7 million in 1952–54.

On the eve of Stalin's death in March 1953, the Gulag had expanded to unprecedented proportions, with the population of both camps and exile settlements at historic highs. In thousands of camps, prisons, and exile settlements across the length and breadth of the USSR, millions of prisoners and exiles toiled and suffered in service to the state. Born during the Stalin Revolution, and subsequently shaped by the Great Terror of 1937–38, World War II, and the intensification of state terror in the postwar era, it became a sprawling state within a state filled with all manner of perceived enemies of the Soviet regime who were judged according to evolving criteria. Although some of its roots lay in the penal system that the Bolsheviks inherited from the Russian empire and in penal experiments of the 1920s, the Gulag was largely a product of the increasingly draconian penal policies of the Stalinist state—a state that ruthlessly punished perceived enemies and criminalized an ever-expanding set of behaviors. While Stalin was alive, there was little chance of the Gulag diminishing in size or importance. Although some of his deputies contemplated minor changes to improve its day-to-day operations, it would not be until after Stalin's death that the Soviet leadership altered the fundamental nature and scale of the Gulag.

Chapter 3
The people of the Gulag

Tens of millions of people came into contact with the Soviet Gulag, whether as prisoners, exiles, perpetrators, or bystanders. Who were these "people of the Gulag"? How did their identities shape their experience, and in turn, how did their experience of the Gulag shape their identities? Although the Stalinist state targeted particular population categories for repression, prisoners and exiles came from virtually every conceivable identity category in the USSR, whether in terms of social class, nationality, religion, gender, sexuality, and age. Most were Soviet citizens, but many were foreigners, whose first experience with Soviet power was the world of imprisonment or exile. The perpetrators, those who worked in the camps as administrators, guards, or civilian personnel, came from a range of backgrounds that was just as broad. Given the Gulag's massive scale and wide distribution across Soviet territory, the bystanders who observed or came into contact with the world of the camps and exile formed the broadest group of all.

The Gulag administration, like the Soviet state in general, sought to continuously categorize members of its subject population as a method of social control, ascribing various markers of identity to each prisoner and exile—what one might call official identity. Inscribed on documents and index cards, this description included not only basic biographical information but also such characteristics as social class, national (or ethnic) identity, and alleged crime. These characteristics, along with assessments of conduct, were supposed to guide how prisoners and exiles were treated. Yet inmates had their own ways of understanding themselves that did not always overlap with how they were described in official documents. This unofficial identity might include loyalties to family, kin, and broader social groups, and also allegiance to a particular category of prisoner identity, whether they saw themselves as "politicals" or members of various criminal groupings. Sometimes, official and unofficial identities overlapped, as was the case with some Ukrainian nationalist prisoners: camp authorities saw them as a threat to the existing order, and the prisoners themselves used national solidarity to resist and undermine various aspects of the camp regime. In many other cases, however, official and unofficial identity clashed, creating potential conflicts between inmate and administration. Ultimately, the victims, perpetrators, and bystanders of the Gulag broadly reflected Soviet society under Stalin, where a state with unprecedented ambitions to categorize and transform society met a diverse population with complex individual and collective identities. While the overwhelming force was always on the side of the administration, state power was nevertheless limited. Thus, prisoners and exiles retained some agency in defining their identity and place in the world of the Gulag.

Rural and urban

The Gulag was an overwhelmingly peasant institution, reflecting the Soviet population at large, which remained predominantly rural until the early 1960s. This was especially true of the "special settlements" to which millions were deported. The first places of exile, created as part of the "dekulakization" of the Soviet countryside in the 1930s, were a cruelly reconstituted version of the villages from which the inhabitants had been deported— villages that were themselves in the process of being transformed by the violence of collectivization. In most cases, peasants were taken from productive land in central regions and relocated to far more marginal agricultural land in Siberia and the North. Although most subsequent deportations of the 1930s, 1940s, and early 1950s targeted populations based on nationality (wholly or in part) rather than class, many victims of later campaigns of violent resettlement came from villages.

Yet the populations of exile settlements in the Gulag were not exclusively from the countryside; urban populations were also exiled. In the 1930s, for example, the secret police experimented with exile as a punishment for urban undesirables (homeless, prostitutes, etc.), sending thousands of urbanites to the North and Siberia. Wartime and postwar deportations from the Soviet Union's western borderlands, aimed primarily at "Sovietization" and pacification rather than at ethnic cleansing per se, also targeted many members of the urban bourgeoisie. Finally, deportation operations that targeted entire national groups during the war sent many urbanites into exile since the goal was to deport entire national categories regardless of where they lived. Needless to say, exiles from urban areas faced severe disadvantages where they were sent, as many completely lacked the skills needed to survive on the land in the Far North, Siberia, and Central Asia.

Like the exiles, most prisoners in the camps came from rural backgrounds. The most famous fictional Gulag camp prisoner, Ivan Denisovich Shukhov, the protagonist of Aleksandr Solzhenitsyn's novella *One Day in the Life of Ivan Denisovich*, was a peasant. Solzhenitsyn chose to write from this perspective not because it reflected his own experience—he was an urban intellectual—but because he wanted to represent the experience of ordinary prisoners. Yet the camp population was, on the whole, more urban than that of the "special settlements." Particularly after the countryside was pacified when peasants were forced to join collective farms in the early 1930s, the state became focused on policing the behavior of city-dwellers. Police presence in cities was far greater than in the countryside, and prosecutions for alleged crimes, whether violent, economic, or "political," were more common. Soviet society itself urbanized rapidly in various waves throughout the 1930s and 1940s, particularly during the Stalin Revolution of 1929–32, which drove millions of peasants into the cities, and after World War II, when millions of demobilized soldiers chose to settle in cities and towns rather than return to their villages. Thus, the rising proportion of prisoners from urban spaces reflected broader changes throughout Soviet society.

Crime: *bytoviki*, "politicals," and "thieves"

The crime for which one received a conviction was another of the most important markers of identity in the Gulag. While exiles were generally given open-ended terms on the basis of their class and/or national identity, prisoners were usually convicted of specific crimes. The type of conviction determined the length of sentences and the type of institution to which they were sent. It was also a key factor determining how they were treated while serving out their sentence. Gulag regulations explicitly called for prisoners to be treated differently depending on their crime and their perceived level of danger to the state. Some prisoners, particularly those convicted of nonpolitical crimes, were prime candidates for *perekovka*, or "reforging." Thus, they could be guarded less carefully and given more opportunities to improve their material conditions in exchange for good behavior. More dangerous prisoners, particularly those convicted of "counterrevolutionary" (political) crimes, posed a higher security risk and were seen as less redeemable. They were supposed to be treated more harshly and have fewer opportunities to improve their material conditions.

Roughly speaking, prisoners were divided into three different categories on the basis of their convictions: *bytoviki*, "politicals," and "thieves." The largest group were *bytoviki*, a term that loosely translates as "those convicted everyday crimes". One of the most important revelations to have emerged from the partial opening of the Gulag archives is that the majority of prisoners were convicted for everyday violations of the Soviet social and economic order. Thus, convictions for theft or lapses in labor discipline (such as illegal job-changing or chronic lateness) were far more common than those for either serious violent crimes or alleged crimes against the state. For example, draconian antitheft laws adopted in 1932 and in 1947 resulted in millions of Soviet citizens being sentenced to long terms of incarceration for petty theft. According to Gulag records, nearly 44 percent of all prisoners held in camps and colonies on January 1, 1951, had been convicted under theft laws, a figure that was approximately double that of those convicted of all "counterrevolutionary" offenses. Long sentences of up to twenty-five years for seemingly minor everyday offenses became especially common after World War II. Thus, the majority of Gulag camp inmates were *bytoviki* who had been harshly punished for relatively minor infractions against the social and economic order.

Prisoners convicted of "political" crimes constituted another substantial group in the camps. From the 1930s through the 1950s, between one-quarter and one-third of the Gulag population were convicted under the section of the criminal code that covered "counterrevolutionary" crimes of various sorts. Such prisoners, who were sentenced for offenses such as "wrecking" (deliberate sabotage of factories), espionage, terrorism, or "anti-Soviet activities" were known variously as "counterrevolutionaries," "politicals," or "58ers" (after the article in the Russian criminal code that outlined such crimes). Most were not prisoners of conscience who had been convicted for genuine attempts to resist the Stalinist order. Although a small minority had actively resisted state power, most never committed a deliberately oppositional act against the Soviet state. Instead, they were ordinary people whose actions had been construed as politically dangerous in an atmosphere of constant suspicion and fear of political enemies. Although those labeled political prisoners had enjoyed special rights in Tsarist prisons, this was not the case in the Gulag. In fact, "politicals" tended to be treated more harshly by the camp authorities and were often looked down upon by other prisoners.

Members of the criminal world, often referred to as "thieves" (*vory*), constituted a third, broad category of Gulag inmates. Often repeat offenders of violent crimes, they belonged to a hierarchy with roots stretching back at least into the nineteenth century (as described in Feodor Dostoevsky's *Notes from the House of the Dead*), with its own rituals, rules, and distinctive argot. Many traditions of these professional criminals were tolerated and even encouraged by Gulag authorities as an informal way to police prisoner behavior. This was largely justified through a class interpretation—as lower-class individuals, professional criminals were considered to be "socially friendly," and so therefore more trustworthy and redeemable than the "counterrevolutionaries." The most elite of the professional thieves, known as the *vory-v-zakone* ("thieves-in-law"), followed a strict code that forbade not only any sort of work in the camps, but also any kind of collaboration with the prison authorities. *Suki* ("bitches"), on the other hand, were willing to collaborate with the state as informants. Making use of an elaborate "reputation system" to maintain status, and adhering to various aspects of a criminal subculture (including language and tattoos), the "thieves" maintained dominance over the general prisoner population throughout the Gulag.

Age and generation

The Gulag population included people of all ages—neither the young nor old were excluded from suffering in prisons, camps, or exile settlements. The age distribution of "special settlers" tended to follow trends in the Soviet population at large, since it was common for entire families to be sent into exile. Younger exiles were more likely to flee, and so therefore the "special settler" population likely had more children and elderly people than the Soviet population at large—although this was to some degree balanced out by the fact that mortality rates were higher among the very young and the very old. Exile itself was experienced very differently by different age cohorts. Numerous memoirs and oral histories recorded in the 1990s and 2000s testify to the degree to which deportation was traumatic for children. For example, 17-year-old Sira Stepanova Balashina was deported with her parents and sister from southwestern Siberia to the Urals region in 1930. Both of her parents and her sister perished during the famine of 1932–33, leaving her alone to make her way in an exile village. Such traumas did not end in early adulthood: her husband, a fellow exile whom she married in the mid-1930s, died at the front during World War II. Although she lived until 2006, Balashina's life was permanently marked by the traumas of exile early in her life.

As is typical for modern prison systems, the population of Gulag camps and prisons tended to be younger on average than the population at large. The age of prisoners clustered around young adulthood, with the very young and the old serving at rates lower than their share of the general population. In 1937, for example, over 70 percent of the prisoner population fell within the age range of 25 to 40. Gulag memoirs and works of literature often focus on the toll that the harsh world of the Gulag took on young prisoners. Young people were not only traumatized by their experiences in the Gulag, but many were corrupted by the harsh world of the camps. Take, for example, the short story "The Artist Bacillus and his Masterpiece" by the Gulag survivor Georgii Demidov, which tells the tragic tale of a young orphan arrested at 14 for counterfeiting and sentenced to a long term in the camps. Blessed with unusual artistic talent, he came under the protection of career criminals, for whom he painted portraits, refusing to work in the camps or collaborate in any way with the authorities. The young artist's work, depicting unrelenting cruelty and death, reflected the corruption and trauma of the world of the camps.

Like many other prison systems, the Gulag operated a separate system of incarceration for young people, with an eye toward preventing the corruption of younger prisoners by their older counterparts. There was a nominally separate system of colonies for prisoners under 18, though it was typically overwhelmed—a March 1941 report noted that with 40 colonies and a capacity for 21,400 prisoners, they were short of 4,000 spaces, meaning that these prisoners would remain in prisons instead. In September 1941 the Gulag administration ordered that those 16 and older could be sent to regular local labor colonies, with the caveats that they were to be held in isolation from adults and that they were to work no more than eight hours per day. Thus, it was not unusual for those under 18 to be imprisoned in regular camps. Furthermore, the special colonies for those under 18 suffered from many of the same problems as regular camps—endemic violence, poor supplies, and lack of oversight.

The Gulag population was also subject to generational shifts that significantly affected the experience of prisoners and exiles. For example, memoirs frequently highlight differences between the prisoners of the 1930s and those who were incarcerated during and after the Second World War. The wartime experience, whether as a combatant or on the home front, was undoubtedly transformative. Beginning in 1939, a large number of new prisoners entered the Gulag who had never before experienced Soviet power, having been arrested in the newly incorporated western borderlands of the Soviet Union. Prisoners and exiles who had fought in the war (regardless of the side), either as official combatants or as partisans, had significant combat experience. The rise in numbers of such prisoners, in addition to the increasing importance of nationality, does much to account for a marked increase in organized prisoner resistance in the postwar era noted repeatedly by camp authorities. The most spectacular manifestations of this resistance were the prisoner strikes of 1953–54 in Norilsk, Vorkuta, and Kengir, yet Soviet archives document a wide variety of organized work disruptions after World War II. Thus, both age and generation were important factors in shaping the experiences of prisoners and exiles alike.

Gender, sexuality, and sexual violence

The Gulag departed significantly from most modern systems of incarceration in that it held a relatively high percentage of women. This was especially true in the "special settlements," where entire multigenerational families were exiled. Although it is difficult to generalize about such villages, it was often the case that they contained significantly more women than men. There was a variety of reasons for this: during "dekulakization" and again during wartime and postwar deportations, adult men were likely to be arrested separately from their families and sent to camps, whereas the rest of the family was deported. Men were also more likely to escape. Finally, conscription from the villages during World War II meant that virtually all able-bodied adult men remaining in the villages were sent to the front or to forced labor elsewhere.

Gulag camps, colonies, and prisons held a smaller proportion of women than the exile villages, but it was nevertheless higher than was typical for most modern penitentiary systems. While women comprised a relatively low percentage of the overall prisoner population in the 1930s (5.9 percent in 1934 and 8.1 percent in 1940), by 1945 they made up 30 percent of the population, before declining to 17 percent in 1951—a rate that was still double what it had been in 1940. This was not simply a relative increase caused by the conscription of men to fight in the war; the absolute number of women in the camps increased 30 percent from 1941 to 1944, and nearly quadrupled in the labor colonies between 1942 and 1944. Such increases are largely attributable to harsh wartime labor decrees that criminalized minor infractions such as

unauthorized job-changing, which disproportionately
affected women.

Many aspects of life in Gulag camps were highly gendered.
Although most camp complexes held both women and men, they
were supposed to be completely segregated from each other to
ensure separation both within the camp living "zone" and in
outside production areas. However, these regulations were
typically undermined in a variety of ways. There was frequently a
shortage of female staff and specialists, so men often worked in
women's sections. Camps rarely built separate infrastructure for
women, meaning that female prisoners often had to be brought
into a male "zone" to obtain food or to bathe. Workplaces were
even less likely to observe strict gender segregation, providing
greater opportunities for interaction. Work in the Gulag was also
determined by sex, with female prisoners more likely to be
engaged in activities thought to be appropriate for women, such as
agriculture or light manufacturing. However, there were notable
exceptions to this: in the coal mining center of Vorkuta, for
example, female prisoners worked underground in one of the
area's mines, though much of the skilled labor and supervisory
staff consisted of male prisoners and nonprisoners.

The Gulag environment, which contained both gender-segregated
spaces and places where interactions between the sexes were
frequent, meant that sex, both heterosexual and homosexual, was
ubiquitous. Judging from archival sources, authorities were far
more concerned about policing heterosexual relationships, largely
because they led to pregnancies and the loss of productivity that
accompanied them. Heterosexual relationships between prisoners
or between prisoners and nonprisoners (euphemistically described
as "cohabitation" in official sources) were forbidden. Yet they were
common enough that authorities nevertheless established special
barracks for pregnant and nursing women throughout the Gulag.
Such facilities, however, provided totally inadequate care for
children—the official death rate in 1947, when the camp system

Alzhir (Akmolinsk Camp for Wives of Traitors to the Motherland)

While the establishment of camps for women often seemed like an afterthought, some Gulag sites were created specifically for female prisoners. Perhaps the best known was Alzhir, or the Akmolinsk Camp for Wives of Traitors to the Motherland. An isolated outpost of the sprawling Karlag system in Kazakhstan, it was established for the sole purpose of holding "wives of traitors of the motherland." This was a new criminal category created during the Great Terror, when the NKVD sought to punish the spouses and children of men convicted of serious political crimes.

Separated from their children, who were imprisoned elsewhere or sent to orphanages, the inmates of Alzhir served sentences of five to eight years purely because of their association with their husbands. Maria L'vovna Danilenko, who was among the first prisoners sent to the camp, described the first summer: "We were put in an old barracks that had initially held exiled kulaks. During the summer the women built 18 buildings: a cafeteria, granary, livestock farms, and a water pump." Eventually, the prisoners built a textile factory, which became the primary economic enterprise in the camp. The work was grueling, especially the manufacture of adobe bricks for construction. Alzhir, like other such camp divisions, was closed in May 1939, and the women were then sent to other camps or labor colonies depending on their perceived level of danger. The fate of children arrested under this order was particularly grim—many remained for years in orphanages, without any information about the whereabouts of their families. Overall, the Alzhir camps are a prime example of how Soviet citizens were punished in the Gulag because of their personal associations with other victims of terror. A museum is now located on the site of Alzhir, a key site of Gulag memory in Kazakhstan.

held more than 15,000 babies, was 409 per 1,000, meaning that over one out of every three babies born in a camp perished. This was over four times the average urban infant mortality in the Russian portion of the USSR from 1946 to 1950. Although the infant mortality rate improved significantly over the next several years, it remained well above the official mortality rate for the Gulag as a whole—and the number of babies born in captivity continued to increase year over year. Attempts to crack down on sexual relations between men and women had little effect, and the only successful method of reducing the number of babies held in the Gulag was through amnesties of pregnant women and those with small children, which happened in 1945, 1947, 1950, and 1953.

While homosexuality clearly violated the sexual rules of the Gulag, same-sex relationships, whether violent or consensual, were nevertheless endemic in what has been described as a "homogenic" system. Much of the culture of same-sex relationships within the camps had roots in the prerevolutionary criminal world, and the massive expansion of the Gulag system unintentionally led to its spread across a much larger penal empire. Such relationships were often overlooked by the authorities since they did not lead to pregnancies and loss of labor productivity. However, there was constant concern about the spread of sexually transmitted infections, and thus Gulag authorities did attempt to police homosexual relationships to a limited extent. Overall, understanding homosexuality in the Gulag is complicated by a dearth of archival sources and the fact that most mentions of homosexual relationships in memoirs reinforce divisions between "politicals" and the criminal "other." In the understanding of most "politicals," sodomy and lesbian relationships were part of the endemic violence and corrupting influence of professional criminals in the camps, precluding the possibility of same-sex intimacy.

Rape and other forms of sexual violence were common in the Gulag, as both nonprisoners and prisoners took advantage of formal and informal hierarchies to terrorize through sex. Left to their own devices for long periods of time, particularly during journeys between penal institutions, there were many opportunities for the strong to prey upon the weak. Gang rape is a major theme in Gulag memoirs and literature. For example, in Tamara Petkevich's *Memoir of a Gulag Actress*, she describes how she was left with a group of prisoners, both men and women, in locked barracks while en route to their final destination. Several male prisoners took the opportunity to rape the female prisoners, and only the fact that one of the prisoners knew Petkevich's husband saved her. Prisoners were frequently pressured into exchanging sex for a greater chance at survival, and Petkevich faced this as well. A male prisoner, the head of the camp cultural educational sector, offered to arrange a transfer from hard labor to a much easier job in his department in exchange for sex. She resisted, but many others entered into such relationships to improve their chances of survival. Yet recent work on sexuality in the camps suggests that some sexual activity in the Gulag was consensual or bartered, offering an opportunity for intimacy and agency for prisoners, albeit within a broader context of extremely limited autonomy. It was an area of "negotiated power" that in some cases allowed the assertion of selfhood and resistance against the existing order. Overall, however, sexual relationships in the Gulag were fraught with violence and coercion.

Nationality, culture, and citizenship

The USSR was a multinational empire that recognized national or ethnic differences, which were accepted, promoted, or repressed depending on the circumstances. Overall, Soviet policy was based on the assumptions that individuals belonged to historically constructed nations and that national groups had the right to limited autonomy within their own national territories. Therefore, it should come as no surprise that nationality was a key marker of identity in the Gulag. In the early 1930s Gulag policies followed the general Soviet approach to non-Russian nationalities.

Assuming that many of the Soviet Union's national groups were more "backward" than Russians, a variety of policies were developed to hasten their historical development. In the Gulag this meant the creation of national minority divisions and brigades in many camps, so that prisoners could work with more familiar conationals and more easily be acculturated to Soviet mores and "redeemed" into law-abiding Soviet citizens. In Dmitlag in the early 1930s, for example, translation bureaus were set up to assist prisoners from national minorities to navigate camp life and the Soviet legal system. This approach, which fit with notions of promoting national differences, was also colonial, emphasizing the importance of "civilizing" members of "backward" national groups, matching stereotypes held by Gulag authorities and prisoners alike.

By the middle of the 1930s, however, the Stalinist obsession with national categories was transformed into fear that the nationalism of some non-Russian peoples posed a danger to the Soviet Union. By 1937 membership in certain national groups was sufficient justification for punishment. Belonging to a suspect national category was the primary criterion used for exile during a series of ethnic cleansing operations that began during the Great Terror of 1937–38 and extended well into the postwar era. By 1941 the Soviet state was practicing full-scale ethnic cleansing against suspect nationalities, attempting to deport the entire nations, such as Soviet Germans, peoples of the South Caucasus, and the Crimean Tatars, into exile in Central Asia and Siberia. Even when nationality was not the exclusive criterion used for punishment, it was increasingly used in conjunction with class, as was the case with the wartime and postwar deportations of populations from Belarus, Estonia, Latvia, Lithuania, Poland, and Western Ukraine.

The national identity of prisoners also became increasingly important during and after World War II. Gulag authorities voiced concern about the activities of prisoners from the Soviet Union's recently annexed territories, especially the Baltic states and Western Ukraine. Such prisoners were not only more common in the postwar Gulag overall, but they became the majority in "special" camps created in 1948 to hold the state's most dangerous prisoners. For example, in Vorkuta's "special" camp Rechlag at the beginning of 1950, a mere 16 percent of the prisoners were Russian, whereas 40 percent were Ukrainian, 12 percent were Lithuanian, 5 percent were Latvian, and 5 percent were Estonian. In the regular Vorkutlag camp, however, Russians still constituted 48 percent of the population. In this context, nationality became the basis for mutual aid networks and organized resistance. Female prisoners from Ukraine, for example, took advantage of the relatively poor supervision of interior camp spaces to transform barracks into familiar domestic spaces as they sought to preserve their identities in the face of camp violence. Mutual aid networks, often constructed on the basis of national identity, became common throughout the postwar Gulag and played a critical role during mass prisoner strikes in 1953–54 in the "special" camps of Norilsk, Vorkuta, and Kengir.

Nationality and language were arguably even more important in the "special settlements." Paradoxically, attempts to punish national groups through mass deportation often had the effect of strengthening national loyalties. Exiled because of their national identity, resettled in national communities, and often segregated from the local population, exiled groups came to rely even more on their common language, culture, and religion for survival in a hostile environment. In the "special settlements," national solidarity was an essential part of survival strategies and network-building. Although Gulag authorities attempted to build informant networks and use state and Party institutions to supersede traditional ties among exiles, they expressed constant frustration at widespread resistance to their efforts. Although some exiles became more assimilated into Soviet life by forming ties outside their national communities, many of the deported national groups closed ranks and became even more suspicious of Soviet institutions.

In the camps, Russian was the common language, and the Gulag was a major site of Russification for prisoners belonging to national minorities. Yet shared language and culture was also an important means for prisoners to preserve their identities in the face of relentless Sovietization. The use of languages other than Russian, while often forbidden, was a way for prisoners to pass on information away from the watchful eyes of the camp authorities. Communicating in one's native language in a letter, even if only for a passage or a short phrase, seemed to carry unusual emotional significance for prisoners and their families on the "outside." Thus, while the camps may have been relentless in pushing prisoners to learn to "speak Bolshevik" (and Russian), various aspects of national identity, language among them, could be an essential method for a prisoner to preserve a sense of self that did not entirely rely on their place in the camp hierarchy.

Although the Gulag was primarily intended to punish and exploit Soviet citizens, the system also held foreign prisoners and exiles. Foreign citizens were relatively few in the 1930s, with 4,475 prisoners without Soviet citizenship held in the camps as of January 1, 1939, approximately one out of every 300 inmates. But Word War II saw a huge rise in the exile and incarceration of foreigners as the USSR swallowed up territories in Poland, Ukraine, and the Baltics. Some of these new Gulag inmates were considered Soviet citizens (against their wishes), whereas others were counted as foreigners. Overall, the largest group of foreigners consisted of POWs, primarily from Germany. Although most foreign POWs were held in a prison camp system that was nominally separate from the Gulag, in practice it was an integral part of the system. Unlike other Gulag prisoners, however, very little effort was made to "Sovietize" or Russify these POWs, since it was always assumed that their economic exploitation would be temporary and that they would return to their home countries at some point in the future. Thus, foreign convicts tended to maintain their language and notion of national identity more strongly than did those who were Soviet citizens.

Gulag "perpetrators"

Prisoners and exiles were not the only "people of the Gulag." The Gulag system also employed tens of thousands of staff to administer the camps, prisons, and exile settlements, serving in a variety of roles, from camp administrators to guards to medical personnel. Remarkably little is known about them individually, largely due to a scarcity of sources. Few personal accounts by Gulag employees have been located, and many official archival materials remain closed. Nevertheless, available sources can tell us some important things about who worked for the Gulag.

The size of the staff employed by the Gulag was enormous, and it grew rapidly alongside the expansion of the system itself. The central apparatus of the Gulag in Moscow alone expanded from 87 employees in 1930 to 1,562 in 1939. Yet it was chronically understaffed at all levels. In the special settlements, it was not unusual for a single commandant to be responsible for all aspects of managing thousands of exiles, including securing supplies, overseeing work, and ensuring security. In the camps, which were set up to constantly monitor and guard prisoners, labor needs were much greater—but were never met. At the end of 1947, for example, there were over 67,000 vacancies for some 324,000 positions in the Gulag system, meaning that more than one in five positions were not filled. Turnover was high due to low pay and poor working conditions—and during World War II a large portion of camp personnel was drafted into the army, leaving the Gulag desperate for workers.

Like any prison bureaucracy, the Gulag was very hierarchical. At the top, the commandants of camps and exile settlements exercised enormous personal authority, with great potential for arbitrariness and corruption. Owing to geographic isolation, a chronic lack of oversight, as well as the intentionally demeaned status of prisoners and exiles, these commandants wielded enormous power over their domains on issues ranging from minutia to matters of life and death. In many respects, they were typical of the "little Stalins" scattered across the length and breadth of the Soviet Union who emulated the patrimonial style of the Soviet leader, with little to restrain them in their management of everyday affairs. Many commandants ruled according to the principle of *edinonachal'e* (one-person rule), with broad responsibility not just for camps and settlements but also for the economic enterprises that they served. With enormous pressures placed on them by Moscow to fulfill regulations and meet production targets under threat of removal or arrest, this created an environment in which violence, arbitrariness, and abuse of position flourished.

Camp guards occupied the opposite end of the hierarchy of Gulag personnel. Many guards, like Ivan Chistyakov, a Muscovite who served as the commander of a militarized guard unit (VOKhR) in BAMlag from 1935–36, were conscripted. Relatively well educated himself, Chistyakov observed that most of the guards he commanded were unruly, uneducated, and totally unprepared for their duties. Violence, arbitrariness, and abuse of power were frequent among guards, not simply because of the power of life and death that they wielded over prisoners, but also because of poor pay, miserable conditions, and low morale. Disciplinary infractions, which included drunkenness, theft, and illegal trade of goods, were common.

Between bosses and guards, tens of thousands of skilled Gulag employees worked in jobs that ranged from surgeon to engineer. Though some of them were trained in schools for camp personnel, many were simply recruited upon graduation from institutions of higher learning, with little choice but to accept their assignment. Transportation engineer Fyodor Mochulsky was thus recruited to work in Gulag camps from 1940 to 1946, where he managed a section of a railroad construction camp. With virtually no preparation, he was put in charge of a camp section with hundreds of prisoners in some of the worst conditions imaginable. In the dead of winter, in the Far North, prisoners were building a railroad, sleeping in the open, and dying in large numbers. As he wrote years later, "But what could two young specialists who had just arrived at the Gulag...what could we actually do?" While such a statement is clearly intended to absolve the author of responsibility for his role in the death of prisoners, it also reflects the degree to which many Gulag staff were simply unprepared for the tasks that they faced.

Overall, what is striking about Gulag personnel is not simply shortages, lack of training, and the proclivity for violence and arbitrariness. Rather, it is their overwhelming "ordinariness." Unlike the staff in Nazi concentration camps, for example, who have often been described as cogs in a highly bureaucratized system, Gulag staff were neither well trained nor efficient in the discharge of their duties. While this by no means absolves them of personal responsibility for their actions, it does help explain the high degree of chaos, corruption, and extraordinary violence that characterized everyday life in camps and exile settlements.

A society of bystanders

In addition to the millions of victims and tens of thousands of perpetrators of the Gulag, there were millions of bystanders, those who observed the Gulag even though they were not directly involved in its day-to-day operations. In his classic study of the Gulag, Aleksandr Solzhenitsyn stressed the degree to which the prisons, camps, and exile settlements were hidden from mainstream Soviet life. Indeed, the operations of the Gulag were shrouded in many layers of official secrecy. While there is little question that very few Soviet contemporaries had clear and comprehensive knowledge of the Gulag's scale, it is also apparent that tens of millions of bystanders had some knowledge of the Gulag, and many encountered it in their everyday lives.

How can we understand the scale of the Gulag's connections to Soviet society and, therefore, the number of bystanders? Millions of prisoners and exiles left behind family, friends, and acquaintances who knew of their disappearance, and in many cases had some degree of knowledge about their whereabouts and the conditions in which they lived. It could be extremely difficult, if not impossible, for loved ones to get accurate information about those who were arrested. Notably, families of those executed during the 1930s were frequently told that those arrested had been sentenced to "ten years imprisonment without right of correspondence," a lie that in many cases was not corrected for decades. Yet many prisoners were nonetheless able to correspond with their families on the "outside" through the official camp mail system or the illegal smuggling of letters. While correspondence on both sides of the barbed wire faced official censorship and self-censorship, some information nevertheless passed through the mail.

Such information also circulated via people living near camps and special settlements. Exiles frequently lived and worked alongside members of existing communities—although the sites of exile were frequently chosen as though they were blank spaces on the map of the Soviet Union, they were often areas with a significant pre-existing population. Thus, secrecy was impossible to maintain. The same was also largely true in the case of camps. Although in theory there were strict regulations and physical barriers in place to separate camps from the outside world, in practice there was a constant flow of people and information into and out of the camps. Many camps were located in close proximity to major cities, including Moscow—and even in very remote areas like Vorkuta and Norilsk, substantial nonprisoner settlements were built on the "outside" that were closely linked to the world on the "inside." While nonprisoners rarely entered the barbed wire "zone," prisoners frequently marched down city streets and worked in factories and other enterprises on the "outside."

All Soviet subjects living in the Stalin era were "people of the Gulag," even as they occupied different positions within this world. Prisoners and exiles came from a broad cross-section of Soviet society in terms of social class, nationality, religion, gender, sexuality, and age. Although the "little Stalins" who lorded over camps and "special settlements" often wielded nearly unlimited authority, most Gulag personnel were remarkably ordinary, poorly trained and not particularly distinguished in terms of their ideological preparation—one factor in creating the violent, but also corrupt and chaotic, world of imprisonment and exile. The broadest category of all, Gulag bystanders, were witnesses (and often participants) in the world of the Gulag because of the proximity of camps and "special settlements" to cities, towns, and villages across the USSR. The Gulag profoundly shaped the experiences of millions of Soviet citizens, albeit in a broad variety of ways.

Chapter 4
Survival, illness, and death

Evfroseniia Kersnovskaia, who spent much of the 1940s and 1950s as a prisoner and exile in various parts of Siberia, was intimately familiar with the physical toll that incarceration took on prisoners. Following an illness that brought her close to death while working on a construction site in the polar city of Norilsk, Kersnovskaia worked in the central camp hospital of Norillag, a sprawling polar camp complex whose primary economic focus was mining nickel and other precious metals. First she was a nurse in the surgical wing, but she was then transferred to an even more challenging role: assistant in the hospital morgue. She found the work profoundly distressing, not least of which because unlike her previous work as a nurse, she was completely unable to help her "patients." Instead, she assisted doctors in determining the cause of death. As she describes in her memoirs:

> Corpses were brought in at any time of day or night, but most often in the afternoon, when I was alone. I often needed to carry them without outside assistance. This was not so hard: corpses from the periphery…—these were the corpses of completely emaciated people. It sometimes happened that I grabbed a pair of unfortunates in my right and left arms and carried them into the morgue without much trouble…The doors of the morgue were always open.

Kersnovskaia's vivid recollections remind us that the Gulag was a system of mass death, where human life was cheap and expendable. Lack of food and overwork meant that prisoners and exiles were caught up in a constant struggle for survival. For prisoners, this was largely a solitary fight, as they lived according to the mantra "you [die] today, but I, tomorrow." This meant relying on whatever advantages they could, even if it resulted in a fellow prisoner dying more quickly. For exiles, survival was a more collective endeavor, as many were able to rely on their families and larger networks for support. At the same time, Kersnovskaia's various camp jobs demonstrate that the Gulag had a relatively well-developed medical system. This system was not, however, oriented toward ensuring quality care for individual prisoners. Rather, it was intended to preserve the overall productive capacity of inmates and return them to heavy labor as quickly as possible. Coupled with constant food shortages and overwork, it might slow the demise of inmates, but it rarely prevented it. Kersnovskaia's story also points to a key aspect of understanding survival, illness, and death in the Gulag: prisoners and exiles had very limited agency in their everyday lives, and thus their chances of survival depended far more on what was done to them rather than on what they could do. Yet Gulag inmates developed a variety of strategies to resist the destructiveness of the system to survive as long as possible.

Food, work, and survival

Prisoners and exiles were chronically underfed and overworked in the Gulag. Survival, therefore, largely hinged on obtaining as much food as possible, while working as little as possible. The USSR suffered from chronic food shortages throughout most of the Stalin era, shortages that were particularly catastrophic during famine (1932–33 and 1946–47) and World War II. Food rationing was common, especially for the USSR's urban population—and most food produced by collective and state farms was sent to the cities, leaving peasants hungry. Prisoners and exiles had even lower priority in the food distribution system, rendering them the most poorly fed populations in the country. Not only were they at the bottom of the official distribution system, but they also had little access to the various means that Soviet citizens used to supplement their diets, which included "private plots" for collective farmers, or for urban-dwellers, private markets and various subsidiary gardens (often run through the workplace). Starvation, and the various illnesses associated with it, was the leading cause of death for Gulag inmates.

In the camps, thoughts of food were all-consuming. According to many prisoner memoirs, food was foremost in their mind from waking until slumber—and even the focus of intense dreams while asleep. Prisoners were typically given three meals per day, and their diet usually consisted of a daily bread ration, watery soup that the prisoners nicknamed "balanda," and thin groats or porridge that was nicknamed "shrapnel." Although there were detailed regulations governing exactly how many calories they were to be given, as well as what their food should contain, in practice the quality and quantity of the food was significantly less than what was prescribed. The fact that prisoners were fed soup ladled from giant cauldrons made it impossible to ensure that each prisoner received an equal share of the ingredients. In practice the thickest portions of the soup, which contained the most nutrients, were given to those favored by the cook who ladled them out.

Even spoons were in short supply in the camps, and so prisoners traded goods to obtain one of their own, a carefully guarded treasure. Because bread was distributed by weight, it often had a very high moisture content, which meant that a higher weight did not necessarily translate into more calories. In the best of times, individual camps rarely received the amount, variety, and quality of food that would have been needed to meet the official quotas. Furthermore, during times of crisis the official ration rates were reduced, particularly during World War II. Thus it should come as little surprise that "nutritional dystrophy," a new Soviet medical term to describe starvation that originated during the Nazi blockade of Leningrad (1941–44), became an increasingly frequent diagnosis and cause of death in the wartime Gulag.

Prisoners attempted to supplement their rations whenever possible. Many prisoners relied on food parcels sent from family to make up precious calories, or to provide them with goods to trade for bread and other essentials. Parcels could rarely be counted upon for a regular food supply given constantly changing regulations, theft by camp officials and fellow prisoners, as well as the changing food situation in Soviet society at large. But goods sent from home could make a significant difference for both physical condition and morale. A 1940 letter from prisoner S. K. Kuskov to his family outlines what was most highly valued in the camps: "fats, sugar, and especially tobacco." He also asked for "onions, garlic... and rolling papers." Prisoners also frequently requested other goods such as clothing, blankets, newspapers, and books, both because of the usefulness of the items and also their value in trade. The camps' informal economy provided other opportunities to supplement one's caloric intake—performing odd jobs for camp officials, guards, or fellow prisoners could net extra bread rations. One should note, however, that whatever a prisoner might gain through informal means had likely been siphoned off

5. This is a camp spoon with the name "Grisha" etched into the handle. Because they were in short supply in the Gulag, spoons were highly prized, and having a spoon with one's name etched on it was a status symbol. The prisoner to whom this spoon belonged likely occupied a privileged position within the prisoner hierarchy.

The Gulag ration system

Prisoners in Gulag camps were fed according to a ration system that tied food to labor output. The 1939 official food regulations provide an example of how such a system was constructed. It included no fewer than 12 different "norms" for prisoners depending upon their job, labor output, and physical health. Each ration included a list of food items and amounts, including bread (the most important component of the ration), flour, groats, meat, fish, fats, potatoes and vegetables, sugar, tea, tomato puree, pepper, bay leaf, and yeast. Bonus rations were given to skilled laborers and prisoners who overfulfilled their production quotas. Prisoners who did not fulfill the plan, as well as those who worked light jobs or not at all (for example, if they were being punished in camp prison) were given significantly less. The Gulag fed prisoners as little as possible while maximizing the amount of labor extracted, necessitating a constant struggle by prisoners to survive.

Prisoners observed that this system hastened physical destruction rather than rewarding higher productivity. In his short story "Shock Therapy," Gulag survivor Varlam Shalamov noted that since rations were not determined by the size of the prisoner, larger prisoners were at a comparative disadvantage. What was worse, the physical capabilities of larger and healthier prisoners made it possible for them to work harder and earn extra rations, at least initially. Yet these bonus rations were rarely enough to compensate for the extra calories expended through work. As Shalamov wrote, "if you wanted to eat better, you had to work better; but if you wanted to work better, you had to eat better." This cycle meant that the healthiest prisoners often succumbed to extreme hunger first. Experienced prisoners like Shalamov concluded that working harder was harmful to one's overall health, even if the reward of extra food was appealing.

from the official camp food supply in the first place. The acquisition of food in the camps was a zero-sum game, and it contributed to conflict and violence among prisoners.

If obtaining more food was essential for survival, so was expending less energy on work. Gulag inmates endeavored to avoid manual labor at all costs, and if assigned such jobs, to work as little as possible. Manual labor, or "general labor" as it was called, often meant exposure to dangers such as extreme cold and unsafe working conditions—but it also meant expending precious energy, and therefore inmates sought to preserve the calories that they consumed by working as little as possible. Prisoners developed a variety of techniques to avoid such work and increase their chances of survival. A hospital stay could provide a reprieve from hard labor, and therefore many prisoners went through extraordinary lengths to be hospitalized. Dissimulation, whereby prisoners attempted to fake an illness or injure themselves to such a degree that they might gain a temporary or permanent reprieve from hard labor, was relatively common. By doing so, however, prisoners not only risked their health but also further punishment, as such acts were often characterized as sabotage and prosecuted accordingly.

Prisoners sought out jobs that were not dangerous or physically demanding, and also those that allowed better access to food and other scarce resources. Each camp required a substantial support and administrative staff engaged in operations such as planning, medical care, food preparation, and providing cultural activities for prisoners and nonprisoners. Not only were these generally low-effort, indoor jobs, but they often offered opportunities to secure extra resources, especially food. Such jobs literally saved the lives of prisoners. Arsenii Formakov, a Latvian writer who was held in Kraslag on the Yenisei River in Siberia, was hired as a weigher of bread rations in 1946, a job that led to an immediate improvement in his physical condition, since it gave him access to extra food. For those who possessed cash or valuables in the camp, more desirable work could be secured via bribes. Specialized training could also help, although that was not necessarily enough to be chosen for the job—there were numerous rules and regulations about who was eligible for many of these positions. Plum job assignments were rarely secure, and they could easily be disrupted by transfer to another camp or changes in the administrative personnel who made these assignments. Yet they were clearly worth the enormous effort and risk often involved in securing them.

Food, work, and the relationship between them played out somewhat differently for exiles. During transportation and in the months immediately after their arrival in exile, food was often in desperately short supply. As in the case of prisoners, the state set ration levels and specified how they were to be supplied. However, exiles rarely received the amount of food specified. Bureaucratic conflict, as well as corruption and general unwillingness to assist socially stigmatized people, further whittled away the food that exiles received during transportation and after arrival. Before they were established in their "special settlements," there was virtually nothing that exiles could do to supplement what the state provided. Lack of food, medical care, and shelter went a long way to explaining the catastrophic conditions and astronomically high mortality rates in the early period after arrival.

Those exiles who survived transportation and the first hungry months in villages provided for themselves as best they could. Exiles assigned to collective or state farms were fed like other members of the rural population, earning a share of the harvest and consuming or selling whatever they could grow on their family's private plot. Given the general level of poverty in most villages after collectivization, such supplies met subsistence needs at best. Those employed in industry earned wages that could be used to purchase food in state stores or in private markets, in addition to having access to other ways that workers were fed in the workplace, which might include workplace canteens or subsidiary agriculture. The "special settlers" found themselves at the very bottom of the food supply system that was both hierarchical and chronically short of supplies. Most were sent to locations with climates that made it difficult to grow potatoes and other foodstuffs on which many Soviet citizens relied for survival. Being uprooted from homes where they had developed social networks was a significant disadvantage, as Soviet citizens often relied on informal ties to make up for deficits in the calories provided by collective farms, the workplace, and state shops.

Exiles often had more agency in their day-to-day affairs than did prisoners, and this was reflected in their repertoire of survival strategies. In many respects, their lives resembled those lived by nonexiles in the regions to which they were sent. Such areas were often very impoverished, but also relatively unsupervised by state officials (beyond the requirement to periodically check in with the commandant). Despite the disruptions of exile, many had relatively strong social networks in their places of exile. Since exile was generally done by family unit, this meant that many could rely on their kin for material and emotional support (although many adult exiles also had the responsibility of supporting children and the elderly and infirm). Some exiles worked to remove the stigmas and legal limitations placed upon them through intermarriage with locals. In this fashion, they increased their chances of survival by forging new ties in their places of exile. Others, however, relied on the opposite strategy, consolidating around national ties to ward off outside influence and "Sovietization" of their community. This was particularly common in the case of the wholesale deportation of nationalities to Central Asia from the South Caucasus and Crimea during the World War II. Although there were deliberate attempts to crush traditional ties in these communities, police reports consistently complained of the persistence of traditional hierarchies and relationships. As groups with long traditions of resisting both Russification and Sovietization, the Chechens and Ingush were particularly vivid examples of how deportations paradoxically strengthened feelings of national solidarity. Thus, exiles relied on different strategies to increase their chances of survival, with some relying on the establishment of new ties in their places of exile, and others seeking to strengthen existing ties with those who came from their own national communities and kinship groups.

Gulag medicine: classification, exploitation, and healing

The Gulag built and maintained an extensive medical apparatus to manage the health of prisoners and, to a lesser degree, exiles. The Gulag's "sanitation department," as it was called, was charged with the task of maintaining the health of inmates and maximizing their labor productivity. It operated according to an apparent paradox—it represented a massive investment in the health of prisoners, boasting tens of thousands of hospital beds (more than 110,000 in 1953) staffed by thousands of doctors, nurses, and other medical personnel (many of whom were themselves prisoners or exiles). Yet the purpose of such a system was not to protect the health of inmates per se but to maximize the capability of each prisoner to work, and particularly to maximize the number who could be assigned to heavy physical labor. This imperative, coupled with the structure of a ration system that was intended to feed prisoners as little as possible while maximizing their labor output, meant that the medical system was an essential part of an apparatus that systematically destroyed the health of its inmates.

Medical professionals, working in concert with production personnel, sorted prisoners and exiles by their physical state to ensure that their labor was maximized. The 1944 regulations stated that prisoners should be sorted into four categories: those "suitable for performing hard physical labor; for moderate physical labor; light physical labor; and 'invalids' who were unable to work." The sorting of prisoners into labor categories was aided by the use of a list of illnesses, which determined how prisoners should be classified depending on a diagnosed ailment and its relative severity. Although such a system was supposed to match inmates with appropriate labor requirements, it privileged insatiable labor needs over health. Industrial managers wielded the most authority in the process, and medical experts often did little more than provide a rubber stamp. Reassessments of labor capacity and health were infrequent, and thus inmates were often worked to the point of physical destruction before they could be reclassified into a less demanding category that matched their physical state. In short, the medical apparatus was a key part of the machinery that resulted in the death or permanent disability of millions of prisoners and exiles.

Despite being cogs in machinery that ruthlessly exploited unfree laborers, medical personnel, many of whom were themselves prisoners and exiles, did have some agency to treat patients and protect them from physical destruction. Prisoner memoirs suggest that while some doctors appeared to show little care, many lives were saved through the personal intervention of medical staff, often at great personal risk. In his short story "Dominoes," Varlam Shalamov's narrator is saved from starvation by a doctor who allows him to remain in hospital for weeks even though he cannot diagnose a specific ailment that would justify his release from work. Often, a chance connection between doctor and patient, such as a common hometown or similar intellectual background, led to an extraordinary intervention. Yet such efforts were possible only on an individual basis, and they were temporary at best—if a prisoner recovered in hospital care, it was very difficult to shelter them from returning them to hard labor.

The camp medical service was one of the few places to find a more lasting (though always tenuous) refuge from the dangers of hard labor. Trained medical personnel were frequently in short supply—although there were some nonprisoners specifically recruited to work in the camp medical service, most positions were filled by prisoners and exiles. This created opportunities for inmates with medical training to work in relative comfort. Rarely, those without previous medical training had opportunities for hospital work. Evfrosiniia Kernsovskaia, who worked in the Norilsk camp morgue, was originally assigned to be a nurse in the surgical ward despite having no previous medical experience or training. Camp medical facilities could also be a refuge for the technically inclined, since medical equipment was frequently in very short supply. Thus the physicist Georgii Demidov built an X-ray machine for the central Kolyma hospital, saving him from "general work" for months. Yet, his case demonstrates just how precarious such positions could be—after completing the machine, he was once again transferred back to the gold mines and his health deteriorated rapidly.

Death and disability

Many prisoners and exiles lost the struggle for survival in the Gulag. For some, death came suddenly from a workplace accident, a bullet from a guard, murder by a fellow inmate, or a brief bout with an infectious disease. For many others, it came after weeks, months, or years of grinding struggle against malnourishment and overwork. Survival techniques might increase one's chances of living longer, but exiles and prisoners had extremely circumscribed agency in their daily lives, and sudden reversals of fortune were common. Some of their graves were marked, but many were hidden. Some prisoners and exiles were buried individually, whereas others were interred in mass graves, like the one discovered in Sandarmokh in Karelia, a northwestern region of Russia, in the late 1990s. The network of burial places, or "necropolis of the Gulag," was spread unevenly across the vast territory of the USSR.

Overall mortality in the Gulag varied enormously over time. It followed national trends, yet the effects of crises on the Gulag population tended to be even more pronounced than they were in the non-Gulag population. In 1936 the prisoner mortality rate in

6. The Sandarmokh cemetery is a memorial site in Karelia, Russia. It was the site of mass executions of prisoners in 1937–38.

the Gulag was likely similar to that of the Soviet Union at large, approximately 20 deaths per thousand. Yet prisoner and exile mortality spiked during the general demographic disasters of the Stalin era, in particular the famines of 1932–33 and 1946–47, and during World War II (particularly 1942–43). Official yearly death rates rose sharply in 1933 at the height of famine throughout the country, reaching 150 per thousand for prisoners and nearly 140 per thousand for exiles—at least three times higher than the official death rates for the USSR as a whole. During World War II, recorded deaths among prisoners reached their highest levels, exceeding 200 per thousand in both 1942 and 1943. By contrast, the recorded deaths rate in Moscow were 34.5 deaths per thousand in 1942 and 24.8 per thousand in 1943. Though the figures for Moscow can hardly be seen as representative of the USSR as a whole, they strongly suggest that Gulag mortality was an order of magnitude larger than that among the civilian population during the war.

Gulag mortality also increased when influxes of new prisoners and exiles strained the system. For prisoners, the largest spike came during the "Great Terror" of 1937–38, which led to an unprecedented number of new arrests that flooded prisons and camps. At the same time, thousands of prisoners were sentenced to death. Overall, the number of deaths recorded in the camps increased over 3.5 times between 1937 and 1938. For exiles, mortality increased dramatically during deportations and during the first few years after arrival when exiles struggled to obtain or build housing and secure a steady supply of food. In 1930, the year that the deportation of "kulaks" began, at least 15 percent of exiles perished. The same was true for subsequent deportations, despite the fact that they were somewhat more centrally coordinated. Nearly 3.7 percent of all Chechens and Ingush died in the first three months of 1945 alone, which was only a year after they had been deported from the South Caucasus. By contrast, the death rate among exiled Soviet Germans, who had been deported in late 1941, was one-tenth of this. Thus, when one was exiled or incarcerated had an enormous effect on one's chances of survival.

The institution to which one was sent also had a significant effect on one's chances of survival. Newly established camps and exile settlements were particularly deadly, with thousands of inmates arriving before there were sufficient supplies and shelter, often in the dead of winter. Perhaps the most shocking example of high mortality among exiles was the so-called "Nazino Affair" of 1933, where more than 6,000 exiles from Soviet cities were dumped on an inhospitable island on the Ob River in Siberia. Within weeks, more than 2,000 of them had died, and dozens of cases of cannibalism and necrophagy were reported. Mortality also varied widely within camp complexes. In Vorkutlag, an Arctic coal mining complex, the official mortality rate for prisoners in 1944 was 49 per thousand. Yet for "hard labor" convicts who were convicted of collaborating with the Germans, it was over eight times higher. In this case, many of the convicts were ill and emaciated before they even arrived—this, combined with the deliberately cruel camp regime, meant that more than one out of every three convicts died that year alone.

Within a particular camp, there were often stark contrasts between the health of individual prisoners. Status and connections were vitally important. Prisoners who were high in the hierarchy of professional thieves were able to avoid work entirely and supplement their diet by preying upon others. Others who managed to secure important jobs with the camp administration were both insulated from "general labor" and often had access to extra food or deficit goods. At the other end of the spectrum, many of the most unfortunate prisoners became "goners" (*dokhodiaga*), the slang term given to the "living skeletons" who were so sick and emaciated that their chances of continuing to survive were slim. Once a prisoner had been reduced to such a state, only an extraordinary intervention like a long hospital stay or a transfer to a convalescence camp offered any hope for recovery.

According to the Gulag's own records, at least 3.7 million exiles and prisoners died from 1929–53: 800,000 executions, 1.7 million deaths in the camps, and 1.2 million deaths in exile. This suggests that roughly 15 percent of prisoners and exiles died over this twenty-five-year period. Yet such figures are incomplete and should be considered minimums. Gulag officials undercounted deaths, struggling to account for the massive flow of prisoners and exiles, particularly during times of significant expansion and upheaval. Also, officials systematically attempted to lower reported death rates by transferring or releasing extremely ill prisoners, thus moving their deaths "off the books." During World War II, such "underreporting" of deaths was not simply permitted but coordinated by Gulag officials. The scale of such underreporting is debated, but one recent estimate suggests that over 800,000 prisoner deaths were hidden through transfer and early release, which would bring the overall figure of deaths from 1929 to 1953 to at least 4.5 million. With approximately 25 million prisoners and exiles serving time in the Gulag during the Stalin era, this suggests that about one out of every five inmates perished. Lack of access to archives, poor record-keeping, and deliberate undercounting make it difficult to quantify Gulag mortality more precisely.

7. Natalia Odyńska and Olgierd Zarzycki, two former prisoners of the Gulag from Poland, stand in front of the watchtower of an abandoned prison camp in Vorkuta, Russia, 1956. Polish prisoners took photographs to document their lives in the USSR while they were awaiting repatriation to Poland. Pictures taken at former camp sites had particular significance, as they were a way to commemorate the Gulag experience.

Physical survival is only one part of the story of how prisoners and exiles endured their terms in the Gulag. Many former prisoners and exiles reported that emotional and spiritual connections were just as essential for survival. Letters from friends or loved ones were particularly important in this regard, providing comfort, information, and connections to those from whom one might be separated for years. Although limited by strict regulations and censorship, many inmates were able to maintain long correspondences utilizing a combination of the official camp postal service and nonprisoner intermediaries who posted letters outside the Gulag, thereby evading at least some limitations and censorship.

Religious observances, whether practiced individually or in a group, was another important way that prisoners and exiles attended to their spiritual well-being. Various religious denominations managed to organize discussions and services, particularly in spaces where it was easier to evade surveillance and denunciation. Exile settlements were even more common sites of group religious worship, given both the frequently lax surveillance of exile communities and the importance of religious ritual in maintaining group cohesion. Not only were underground religious services led by exiled clerics, but other forms of religious organization persisted, including religious "brotherhood" organizations among Muslims. Sustaining friendships formed in the Gulag, although this was, according to survivor Varlam Shalamov, only possible "in difficult but bearable conditions," rather than in life-threatening ones. Prisoners and exiles found many ways to resist the rules of a system that sought to destroy them both physically and psychologically.

Overall, survival was much more common than death in the Stalinist Gulag. Yet the likelihood of a prisoner or exile surviving depended above all else upon circumstances and the conditions to which they were subjected. In certain moments and locations, death was far more likely than survival. On the other hand, in established camps and exile settlements, outside of crisis years, mortality was not much greater than that of the Soviet population outside the Gulag. Thus, while Gulag inmates deployed a variety of strategies to help their chances of survival, whether they lived or died mostly depended on circumstances far beyond their control.

Discussions of survival and death cannot adequately address the question of how the experience of the camps affected survivors in physical and psychological terms. Forced labor in inhumane conditions permanently affected the health of millions of survivors. Cold, malnourishment, overwork, and infectious diseases took an enormous toll. Many were permanently disabled, and even those whose health was not seriously affected experienced chronic illnesses for the rest of their lives. The psychological traumas of incarceration, violence, displacement, and routine exposure to death affected millions of survivors as well. Such wounds extended beyond inmates themselves to a far broader swath of the Soviet population, whether it was family and loved ones, perpetrators, and the bystanders who witnessed Gulag institutions in their midst. Thus, the Gulag stands alongside the famines of 1932–33 and 1947–48, and World War II, as the greatest human tragedies experienced by the Soviet population in the Stalin era. Although the suffering inflicted by the Gulag was very unevenly distributed, it was widespread.

Chapter 5
Economics and labor
in the Gulag

Julius Margolin, a Jewish-Polish prisoner who was sent to the White Sea-Baltic Canal camp complex at the beginning of World War II, worked for a time as the secretary to a camp section boss. As part of his duties, virtually every piece of camp paperwork passed through his hands. Of the information and language that he encountered in these documents, one particular formulation stuck out to him: *rabguzhsila*. It was a portmanteau that combined two measures of labor power: human labor power (*rabsila*) with horsepower (*guzhevaia sila*). According to Margolin, "The word...joins people and animals together for work tasks and equates them in dignity, value, and destiny." In highlighting this turn of phrase in his memoir, Margolin emphasizes the dehumanization of prisoners and their treatment as units of production. It is also a striking reminder of the overwhelming importance of labor, and of economic considerations, throughout the Stalinist Gulag.

The Gulag was unusual among modern penal systems in its emphasis on forced labor and production results. Economic concerns played a central role in determining the overall structure of the system, the geography of penal institutions, and the nature of daily life within the camps and exile settlements. Stalin and his closest advisors saw the Gulag as a tool for development that could be used for all manner of economic tasks, and they believed it was particularly well suited to extracting resources and building infrastructure in far-flung places where labor was scarce. The idea that cheap forced labor could offset the cost of incarcerating millions and therefore make the Soviet penal system economically self-sufficient was also central to its functioning—although it was never borne out in practice, the notion nevertheless endured from the 1930s until the 1950s. In both abstract regulations and the minutiae of everyday life, the Gulag system was set up to maximize the extraction of labor power from each inmate and contribute it toward the Soviet economy. While it coexisted with other goals, such as punishment, isolation, and rehabilitation (or "re-forging"), economic exploitation was one of the most important organizing principles of the Gulag.

As an economic system, the Gulag presented constant challenges to its managers. Despite the persistent notion that Gulag labor was cheap and that penal institutions could become self-sufficient, it was incredibly inefficient and wasteful of human life (not to mention other resources). A system of graduated rations that depended upon physical condition and labor output led to a constant degradation of prisoner health and was not sufficient to exhort healthy prisoners to work harder. The fact that the Gulag's leaders periodically attempted to introduce additional incentives such as wages or early release opportunities demonstrated that these fundamental issues were never resolved in the Stalinist Gulag. And like the Soviet economy at large, inefficiencies in the "official" economy led to the development of a robust "second" economy that included a range of activities such as sales of contraband products and attempts to manipulate production figures. These adaptations may have helped sustain individual prisoners and the system itself, but at the same time they undermined attempts to transform the Gulag into a productive sector of the Soviet economy.

The Gulag in the Soviet economy

In the early 1920s, the chief of the Soviet secret police (Cheka) Feliks Dzerzhinskii proposed two key ideas that would become central to the Gulag and its place in the Soviet economy. First, he declared that prisoners "must cover their expenses with their labor," so that the Soviet carceral system could be cost neutral. Although the Gulag system never achieved economic self-sufficiency, the idea that unfree labor would pay for itself became a key element of the Gulag in the 1930s and remained remarkably persistent throughout the Stalin era. Second, Dzerzhinskii argued that prisoners could be used for the "colonization of uninhabited areas" in the USSR. This statement was consistent with a widely shared idea among Bolsheviks that the state could overcome the "backwardness" of regions and peoples through economic development—while denying agency to those peoples who were the objects of such efforts. Dzerzhinskii proposed that the carceral system would be a tool for colonization, building the infrastructure and enterprises needed to settle remote areas, while also providing the long-term population. Although these ideas were not widely implemented in the 1920s, they guided Soviet penal policy as the number of prisoners and exiles rapidly increased during the first five-year plan (1928–32). The Politburo endorsed the OGPU's proposal that both "corrective labor camps" and "special settlements" be used as institutions that could harness unfree labor to advance the state's economic goals with an eye toward both self-sufficiency and long-term colonization.

As part of the Stalin Revolution and its twin projects of transforming Soviet agriculture and industry, Stalin and the Politburo approved the widespread use of exile and prisoner labor. Gulag labor was widely used in large-scale capital construction, particularly of dams, canals, and railroads. These projects provided an ideal opportunity for leaders of the early Gulag to demonstrate the economic potential for labor camps. The White Sea-Baltic Canal project, intended to build a continuous waterway between Leningrad and Arkhangelsk, was the first Gulag megaproject, completed from 1931 to 1933. Following its completion, the Gulag was entrusted with other large infrastructure projects such as the Moscow-Volga Canal, the

Baikal-Amur Mainline (a northern spur of the Trans-Siberian Railway), and, after World War II, the "Great Constructions of Communism," which included canals, hydroelectric stations, and irrigation projects. By early 1941, the Gulag's economic activities had become so complex that oversight was split into a series of economic administrations, each of which managed its role in a particular sector of the economy. In 1952, on the eve of Stalin's death, the Gulag received more than 10 percent of all capital investments in the Soviet Union, more than any other ministry, demonstrating that it had become the most important construction agency in the Soviet Union.

The Gulag was also assigned mining projects, particularly those in remote locations with few workers and little of the infrastructure needed to attract more. The largest and most important of these was Dalstroi, established in November 1931 for the purpose of mining gold and other precious metals on the Kolyma River in the far northeast. It eventually became the largest camp complex in the USSR, with over 200,000 prisoners by the early 1950s. It, like many other camps, was run according to the principle of *edinonachal'e* (one-person rule), with a single director given broad responsibility over virtually every aspect of life in the region. This model was followed in the establishment of other extraction enterprises, including a coal mining center in Vorkuta and a nickel mining complex in Norilsk. Natural resource extraction became one of the Gulag's central economic activities, and it accounted for a significant portion of the country's extractive enterprises, particularly of nonferrous metals.

Forestry was another economic sector where the Gulag played an outsized role. Lumber had been one of the key economic activities of the Solovki camps in the 1920s, and it remained so as the Gulag expanded. By 1932, there were six Gulag camps whose primary economic task was producing lumber, representing nearly 10 percent of the entire Soviet lumber sector. The Gulag's share in

Belomorkanal

The White Sea-Baltic Canal, also known as Belomorkanal, was the first large infrastructure project built by the Gulag. The canal linked the White and Baltic Seas, providing an improved transportation route between Leningrad and Arkhangelsk. Eager to demonstrate the potential of its labor force, the Gulag leadership mobilized more than 120,000 prisoners on the worksite of the project, representing one quarter of the total number of prisoners in the Gulag. The canal was completed in twenty months from 1931 to 1933, a seemingly spectacular result.

Belomorkanal was used to extol the virtues of the new Soviet approach to prisoner corrections both at home and abroad. The project garnered extensive coverage in the official Soviet press, and Maksim Gorky, a preeminent literary figure, was enlisted to produce a volume commemorating the construction. The resulting book included work by Gorky and other artists like the writer Mikhail Zoshchenko and the constructivist photographer Aleksandr Rodchenko. These appeared alongside prisoner testimonies. However, Belomorkanal was the last major Gulag project to be discussed in the public record—after its completion, references to Gulag projects in print were scant and clouded in obfuscation.

Belomorkanal was a testing ground for many of the principles of the early Gulag system. Very little mechanization was used; workers moved enormous amounts of earth by shovel and wheelbarrow. The loss of life on the canal was enormous: according to official statistics, over 12,000 prisoners died during its construction, although this was undoubtedly an undercount, especially considering that it was completed during a deadly famine. The finished canal was virtually useless: in order to speed up construction, the depth was set at only 10 to 12 feet, making freight shipping impossible. Yet the results convinced Stalin that the Gulag was a viable economic model, and thus the use of forced labor continued to spread thereafter.

8. Prisoners mine gold in Kolyma, Russia, 1941–44. The figure in the middle dressed in dark clothing is likely a guard or an overseer. Gold mining was one of the most important economic activities in the Gulag, as the USSR traded gold for machinery and other prized foreign goods.

the lumber industry grew in the 1930s and 1940s, as the promise of cheap and mobile labor seemed to be a good solution for an industry that perpetually struggled to meet plan targets. These camps had some of the worst conditions throughout the Gulag, owing to their remoteness, the brutal nature of tree felling work, and the fact that they moved regularly as forests were depleted. On the eve of Stalin's death in 1953, the forestry camps held more than 10 percent of the total prisoners in Gulag camps, the third highest total for a specific sector of the economy.

Although most prisoners were employed directly in Gulag enterprises, many were instead contracted out to other economic ministries, particularly in defense production. Under this arrangement, prisoners were held in camps but traveled to factories to work alongside nonprisoners. In return, such industries were supposed to pay the camps for the labor provided, payments that would provide for the prisoners' upkeep. The Gulag's role in providing contract labor grew during

World War II. Camps in the area surrounding Novosibirsk provided tens of thousands of prisoners as contract labor to the defense industries concentrated in the city. Such labor continued to be important after the war, and in the end of 1947 nearly one-quarter of the prisoners in the Gulag were contracted to outside industries.

While the Gulag tended to be used for economic activities that required large amounts of unskilled labor in remote locations, it also played a key role in the design and production of high technology. Technological development in the Gulag was typically concentrated in camps known as "sharashki" (singular, *sharaga* or *sharashka*, a slang word for a criminal organization), as described in Solzhenitsyn's novel *In the First Circle*. The best-known of these was design bureau TsKB-29, a camp associated with Andrei Tupolev, who had been the chief aviation engineer in the USSR until his arrest in 1937 for alleged sabotage and espionage. Such camps held arrested designers and engineers from across the USSR, and the NKVD periodically searched the Gulag population for qualified personnel who could join them. Located close to major population centers, such camps held prisoners in relative comfort, with an ample food supply and the guarantee of avoiding dangerous manual labor. Prisoners in the sharashki typically worked alongside nonprisoners, which afforded increased opportunities to have contact with the world outside the camps. Although such camps existed from the 1930s to the early 1950s, they played a particularly important role in developing weapons of war, including the Tu-2 and Pe-2 aircraft that were key to Soviet victory in World War II. The apparent success of these camps in developing technology meant that coercion and secrecy shaped the Soviet scientific and engineering sector after Stalin's death.

Unlike prisoners, exiles were not typically used in high priority projects like canal construction or scientific development. However, the Gulag deployed exile labor for a range of economic activities throughout the USSR. Although adult exiles were required to work as part of their punishment, they generally did not work directly for enterprises that were part of the Gulag economic empire. Rather, they were used as a pool of unfree labor for agriculture and industries in the regions to which they were exiled. Particularly in the 1930s, this meant working in timber industries. In the vast Urals region of central Russia, demand for labor in forestry seems to have driven the repression of peasants, as Party and industrial bosses became so desperate to meet production targets that they demanded ever greater numbers of unfree laborers be sent from peasant villages. Many other exiles, particularly those who were sent to Central Asia during and after World War II, were assigned to collective or state farms. This constituted the Gulag's largest role in Soviet agriculture, although many Gulag camps maintained small agricultural enterprises to help feed prisoners. Finally, many exiles, particularly adult males, were assigned to work in industrial enterprises. In the steel town of Magnitogorsk, thousands of men endured forced labor at the worksite. One such "kulak" exile, Shabkov, figured prominently in American John Scott's memoir about his time building a Soviet steel plant in the 1930s, *Behind the Urals*.

Just as the use of Gulag labor spread throughout many sectors of the economy, it also expanded throughout the territory of the Soviet Union. Given the notion that prisoners and exiles could be used to "colonize" the USSR, it should come as no surprise that many camps and special settlements were located in more sparsely populated regions of the country, particularly in areas with extreme climates such as the Far North, Siberia, and the Central Asian steppe. Gulag institutions were frequently concentrated within particular regions, rendering them an essential part of regional development, leaving a legacy that survived long after Stalin's death. Nearly every city in Komi ASSR, a region in the northeastern part of European Russia, was built by prisoners alongside a camp complex. And while central planners may have chosen locations for camps and exile settlements in areas that they perceived to be empty, the people already living in such areas were not always pleased to have inmates in their midst. The concerns of indigenous populations were typically ignored by Gulag planners, and they were frequently displaced by camp complexes.

For all its association with developing far-flung areas, prisoners and exiles were also concentrated around key industrial regions and urban areas. Perhaps the most vivid example of this was the Western Siberian city of Novosibirsk and its environs, which was covered in a patchwork of exile settlements and camps, particularly during and after World War II. Moscow itself saw a large concentration of camps, and tens of thousands of prisoners built the central structure of the new Moscow State University campus, one of several distinctive "Stalin skyscrapers" raised in the late 1940s and early 1950s. Thus, while the geographic footprint of the Gulag tended to be concentrated in certain pockets of Soviet territory, camps and exile settlements were not confined to the periphery.

How can we measure the overall contributions of the Gulag to the Soviet economy? It was, quite obviously, an area of significant investment. At its height during World War II, the share of forced laborers in the USSR reached nearly 10 percent of the total workforce. Although this was a high proportion, it was significantly lower than in Nazi Germany, where forced laborers represented over one-quarter of the total workforce by 1944. Yet despite the relatively large number of forced laborers, historians and economists have generally concluded that the contributions of the Gulag to the Soviet economy were minimal. The exile of millions of peasants and members of national minorities caused enormous economic disruptions in their home regions while offering little to no gain where they were forced to resettle. The notion that prisoner and exile labor was completely mobile and extremely cheap encouraged wasteful investment in remote regions. Thus, while the Gulag was an area of significant cost and investment by the Soviet state, it gained very little economic benefit from it—representing yet another area where prisoners and exiles suffered in vain.

The internal economics of the camps

Gulag camps were run as economic units according to the principles of Soviet planning. Much of the organization revolved around the fulfillment of production targets, and responsibility for fulfilling them was broken down into ever smaller units: camp sections or "points," prisoner brigades, and individual prisoners. While such considerations were not the only logic governing the operations of camps, they played an unusually large role. At its core, the economics of the individual camp was based on the involuntary exchange of prisoner labor for food rations. Although the exact origins of this system are debated, historians agree that its use began in the Solovki camps of the late 1920s, when Naftalii Frenkel, a former prisoner turned supervisor, implemented reforms to improve prisoner productivity. During his tenure, two key changes were introduced in the organization of prisoner labor: prisoners were classified according to their ability to work, and they were given rations that corresponded to their labor output, so that prisoners who produced more received more food. The size of prisoners' rations was determined according to a complex formula that took into account a variety of factors, including a prisoner's health status, the type of labor performed (favoring skilled and heavy physical labor), and the location of the camp (favoring those in extreme geographic environments). Most importantly, prisoners were "rewarded" with food on a sliding scale depending upon what percentage of the plan they fulfilled. Such regulations were intended both to punish poor performance with smaller rations and reward exceptional production with bonuses above the baseline.

The 1939 food regulations demonstrate these principles at work in determining the size of bread rations, which were the largest part of each prisoner's diet. Prisoners who did not work or produced less than 60 percent of the plan received 600 g of bread, whereas those who fulfilled their work quotas received 1,200 g; those who exceeded their quotas were given 1,400 g; engineering and technical personnel earned 1,500 g. Prisoners on punishment rations, on the other hand, received only 400 g. Such ration regulations should not be mistaken for an actual reflection of the food that prisoners were able to consume, which was invariably lower than the official rations. As a system to increase production, it did so more by punishment than by rewards—the marginal increases for beating plan targets were generally much lower than the penalties for falling short. Further, plan fulfillment was usually calculated by brigade rather than for individual prisoners. As in so many other aspects of life in the Soviet Union, the goal was to use the principle of collective responsibility to exhort the prisoners to produce more, leaving the punishment of individuals who did not do their part to each brigade. It also placed enormous pressure on brigade leaders to ensure that their brigades fulfilled quotas so that all members could be fed adequately.

Gulag authorities were rarely satisfied with the incentives created by this ration system, and so they frequently experimented with other ways to improve prisoner productivity. These consisted primarily of material incentives and credit for early release. Throughout the 1930s and 1940s, prisoners could earn monetary rewards for plan fulfillment, though the payments were very small. By the late 1940s, Gulag administrators acknowledged that the rewards were inadequate to encourage productivity, and so they introduced a full-blown system of prisoner wages that was eventually extended to all working prisoners in the early 1950s. Although the wages were considerably lower than those paid to nonprisoners, they often provided prisoners the opportunity to purchase food in camp stores to supplement their rations. Workday credits, which rewarded productive work with a credit for extra time served, were offered selectively throughout much of the 1930s and then reintroduced widely beginning in 1948. The introduction of wages and reintroduction of workday credits in the late 1940s and early 1950s were a tacit acknowledgement by Gulag authorities that prisoner productivity was extremely low.

Overall, prisoners in the highest priority camps were the most likely to benefit from such incentives, and they were unevenly distributed within the camps themselves, often reinforcing existing prisoner hierarchies.

However, one cannot understand the economics of the Gulag based solely on formal rules and structures—there were also many informal practices that were endemic in Soviet places of confinement. As was the case across the Soviet Union, there was a vibrant "second" (unofficial) economy that compensated for shortcomings in the official economy. Falsification of production data was widespread. The slang term for this, *tufta*, first appeared in a 1927 dictionary of prisoner language published in the Solovki camp as part of a collection gathered by the imprisoned historian and ethnographer Nikolai Vinogradov. Brigade leaders habitually practiced *tufta* to ensure that their brigades met the plan and received adequate rations. A tree-felling brigade might pad its numbers to meet or exceed a production quota that could not otherwise have been met. They might try to count trees twice or clean off logs felled previously so that they appeared to be newly chopped. As was the case across the Soviet economy, chronic shortages of supplies and an overreliance on quantitative indicators incentivized such schemes—and the graduated ration system rendered it a matter of life and death. *Tufta* was ubiquitous and was not simply practiced by prisoners—camp officials, from local camp section chiefs all the way up to the central Gulag administration in Moscow, attempted to improve results and avoid punishment by inflating production figures. Although it was generally unavoidable, getting caught could have significant consequences, so skilled practitioners of *tufta* endeavored to keep the practice within limits to lower the risks of getting caught punishment.

Other "second economy" activities included the trade of goods, especially intoxicants (tobacco, tea, and alcohol), food, and clothing. Goods acquired outside the camps, whether they were brought in by the prisoners themselves or mailed in packages, naturally had a higher value than camp-issued items. As in many prison environments, the basic unit of value tended to be expressed in easily exchangeable units, such as cheap tobacco (*makhorka*), bread rations, or tea. Cash rubles were also exchanged depending on their usefulness—the wage reform of the late 1940s meant that more cash was in circulation, and since they could be spent within the camp, more desirable. Violence was often involved in such transactions—a prisoner might simply have a prized good seized by others in the barracks. Often, guards and camp officials played a part in the trade by supplying rare and valued goods like alcohol. In particularly desperate economic periods, camp guards were even known to trade camp goods in surrounding settlements.

As in Soviet society at large, informal economic practices were intimately related to the official economy. When they were able, prisoners made use of official privileges and positions to profit from the informal economy, and vice versa—a practice generally known as *lapa* ("paw") in camp jargon. A classic demonstration of this practice comes from Varlam Shalamov's short story "The Typhus Quarantine." In this story, which is set in massive barracks where prisoners were being held under quarantine, the seemingly humble position of "sanitation man" presented many valuable opportunities for personal enrichment. Because the sanitation man was the only prisoner allowed to leave the quarantine barracks, it was lucrative, since he could bring goods into the camp from the outside for trade. As Shalamov related in his laconic style, "Ognev offered his jacket and the fiber suitcase to the supervisor and got the job of the deceased sanitation man. About two weeks later, criminal convicts tried to strangle Ognev in the dark—fortunately, they didn't kill him—and took about 3,000 rubles off him." Thus, an opening in a valuable position presented an opportunity for the supervisor to take a bribe, for an ordinary prisoner to earn money through illicit trade, and for the criminal elite to shake down the prisoner for a handsome profit.

The Gulag's emphasis on labor was one factor ensuring that camps and exile settlements were never as isolated from the "outside" as security regulations stipulated. While some prisoners worked inside the enclosed space of the "zone," most worked on the outside, taken to and from the camp every day via a guard convoy. Depending on their job and location, this might present opportunity for occasional or regular interactions with nonprisoners. Prisoners provided under contract to other industries often worked alongside nonprisoners in factories or at construction sites. Although a guard detail usually supervised prisoners at work, this was not always possible. In the coal mines of Vorkuta, for instance, prisoners frequently worked unsupervised alongside nonprisoner specialist and supervisory personnel, offering plenty of opportunities for the exchange of information and goods. In many camps, select prisoners known as "pass-holders" (*propuskniki*) were given passes that conferred the privilege of moving around outside the camp unguarded. More rarely, some prisoners were even allowed to live outside the camp "zone" itself. Aleksei Kapler, a major Soviet filmmaker before his arrest, was allowed to live in a photo hut in the city of Vorkuta, outside the grounds of the camp, so that he could carry out his duties as city photographer. Although security and economic concerns frequently came into conflict in the day-to-day operations of the camps, the imperative for each brigade, section, and camp to meet production targets necessitated less than complete isolation of many prisoners.

Assessing the Gulag economy

In many important respects, the economy of the Gulag was a reflection of the Stalinist economy as a whole. The Gulag's economic empire extended into nearly every sector, from agriculture to mining to construction, though big infrastructure projects and natural resource extraction were clearly favored. Prisoners and exiles worked in virtually every corner of the vast Soviet space, although economic activities tied to the Gulag tended to be concentrated in clusters located in both remote areas and major cities. Like other parts of the Soviet economy, the Gulag was neither subject to market forces nor to meticulous planning—rather, it was oriented toward meeting production targets. It relied on rewards for meeting quotas and punishments for falling short. This system of rewards and punishments reached from the central administration down to the level of the prisoner brigade, and ultimately, the individual prisoner. As in other sectors of the economy, informal economic practices such as *tufta* and an active second economy emerged to compensate for structural inefficiencies and gaps.

The Gulag economy also reflected the Stalinist economy's reliance on coercion to an even greater degree than elsewhere. For Stalin and his closest advisors, coercion was what rendered the Gulag such a powerful economic tool. Camps and exile settlements could be built wherever there was a perceived economic need. Prisoners and exiles could be dispatched there with the stroke of a pen. The camps themselves were organized according to clear rules and hierarchies, ensuring efficient management. Thus, the Gulag was the ideal tool for colonization of the Soviet hinterland, and for the transformation of nature to serve the needs of the state. Whereas other parts of the Stalinist economy were marked by chaos, massive labor turnover, and shortages, Gulag projects offered rationality and order at a low cost—even if they never delivered on such promises. The centrality of labor exploitation to the Gulag has led many survivors and scholars to call inmates slaves, suggesting that the Gulag is best understood as a system of slavery. Although this characterization tends to overlook that the Gulag was a penal system, which also emphasized punishment, isolation, and the possibility of rehabilitation or "reforging," it is useful in that it captures two key elements of the Gulag's nature: the overwhelming focus on economic exploitation and the extreme debasement (legal or otherwise) of the system's inmates.

The Gulag also suffered from many of the shortcomings of the Stalinist economy and, ultimately, exposed the clear limits of coercion as an economic tool. Gulag projects were extraordinarily wasteful, both in terms of human life and other forms of capital. This was true from its inception, as in the case of the White Sea-Baltic Canal project of the early 1930s. Although it was lauded as a resounding success, a minimum of one-tenth of the prisoner population died during the twenty months of construction and vast resources were expended, all to build a canal that was of almost no economic utility. Despite the notion that Gulag labor was cheap from an economic standpoint, it proved to be extremely unproductive. Periodic experimentation to improve this productivity through incentives such as wages and early release failed to produce significant improvements. Therefore, it is unsurprising that Stalin's successors implemented a wide range of economic reforms to the Gulag immediately following his death in March 1953.

Chapter 6
After the Stalinist Gulag

The use of mass repression by the Soviet state against its citizens did not survive Stalin's death. The dictator died at his country house on March 5, 1953, without having named an heir. After a brief leadership struggle, Nikita Khrushchev, who had occupied a variety of top leadership roles under Stalin, outfoxed potential rivals to become the uncontested leader of the USSR. As he maneuvered, Khrushchev also embarked upon a dramatic transformation of the system of prisons, camps, and exile settlements. He significantly reduced the size of the prisoner population and ended the use of mass exile as a punishment for specific class or national groups. In addition to being much smaller, the post-Stalin Gulag was no longer a massive economic enterprise, as the emphasis shifted toward rehabilitation rather than exploitation. Khrushchev, and Leonid Brezhnev, who assumed power after Khrushchev was deposed in 1964, ensured that the Gulag was no longer a place of mass punishment for perceived political foes of the state. Although the state continued to incarcerate a significant number of political dissidents in a network of camps and psychiatric hospitals, from the end of the 1950s the system more closely resembled the prison systems of other modern states that sought to isolate, punish, and rehabilitate those deemed to pose a danger to society.

Reforms to the Gulag in the 1950s and 1960s meant the rapid release of millions of prisoners and exiles back into Soviet society.

What followed was an unprecedented social experiment: could Soviet society reintegrate former prisoners and exiles successfully, and could those released navigate a successful return to civilian life? This mass return was far from a smooth process because of widespread suspicion of, and prejudice against, former prisoners and exiles. State policies were woefully incomplete and contradictory. Former prisoners and exiles and their families worked to process their experiences in the Gulag, leading to the development of a small but growing corpus of Gulag literature and memoirs. Aside from a brief period in the early 1960s, public discussion and memorialization of the Gulag were not officially allowed, but by the late 1980s the state's embrace of the policy of *glasnost'* ("openness") opened the floodgates to an outpouring of efforts to come to terms with the Gulag and its legacy.

Discussions and efforts to determine the Gulag's place in history and memory became even more fragmented after the collapse of the USSR in 1991. Conflicts between state actors and various constituencies continued, yet they were also profoundly shaped by efforts in each successor state to build a new national identity. In some countries, such as Estonia, Latvia, and Lithuania, denouncing Stalin's crimes and the Gulag became part of a broader rejection of the Soviet period as an illegitimate imperial project. In others, including Russia, efforts to study and memorialize the Gulag came into conflict with state myths that glorified many aspects of the Soviet era. The memory of the Gulag became enmeshed in debates about the meaning and legacies of the Soviet project. The fate of the institutions of incarceration raised another set of questions about the Gulag's long shadow: how did the legacies of the Stalinist system affect the prison systems in the USSR and the post-Soviet states?

Reform and "socialist legality" in the Gulag after Stalin

Stalin's rule and the Gulag were inseparable. Once he died, however, his inner circle wasted little time in launching sweeping changes to the system that Stalin had overseen. The triumvirate that assumed power in the immediate aftermath consisted of Lavrentii Beriia, head of the vast state repressive apparatus, including the secret police and camps, Georgii Malenkov, chair of the Council of Ministers of the USSR, and Khrushchev, head of the Communist Party. Although all three had been deeply involved in the machinery of mass repression, they agreed that reforms were necessary to secure the goodwill of the general population at a time of great instability. A mere three weeks after the dictator's death, on March 27, 1953, the government announced a broad amnesty of prisoners that resulted in the release of more than 1.2 million of the approximately 2.4 million prisoners in camps and colonies over the next several months. Although it had much in common with previous amnesties, as it primarily targeted categories of unproductive prisoners such as the old, young, pregnant, and terminally ill, those given short sentences and convicted of official or economic crimes were also released. Those convicted of "counterrevolutionary" crimes, major theft, and violent crimes were excluded—but the scale of the amnesty was nonetheless unprecedented. The amnesty was followed by the cancellation of several massive infrastructure projects being built by prisoner labor and a change in the oversight of the camp system. To a large degree, these were reforms that had been worked out before Stalin's death but had been impossible to implement while he was alive.

Those prisoners who remained in the camps were encouraged by the 1953 amnesty but frustrated at their exclusion. The amnesty, along with other reforms, created a crisis of increased expectations among the more than 1 million prisoners left behind barbed wire. In 1953–54 the Gulag experienced three major prisoner uprisings, each of which took place in a "special camp" where most prisoners had been convicted of "counterrevolutionary" crimes. Strikes in Gorlag (Norilsk) and Rechlag (Vorkuta) in the summer of 1953, and a strike in Steplag (Karaganda, Kazakhstan) in the summer of 1954 saw tens of thousands of prisoners demand improved conditions, better treatment, and reconsideration of their cases.

The leadership of each of the three strikes had a high representation of Red Army veterans and former nationalist rebels from the western borderlands (Ukraine and the Baltic states) who had actively resisted Soviet power. The last of the strikes, in Steplag, lasted forty days. Each mass uprising ended with bloodshed as the camp authorities opened fire on prisoners who refused to return to work. Nevertheless, the Soviet state did send high-level officials to negotiate with the prisoners.

After Beriia was arrested for alleged espionage in June 1953 and Malenkov was forced to resign in January 1955, Khrushchev emerged triumphant in the struggle to succeed Stalin as General Secretary of the Communist Party. He continued to transform the Gulag as part of a broader campaign to restore "socialist legality" in the USSR. His government largely dismantled the vast system of internal exile, which had held approximately 2.8 million people in exile at the time of Stalin's death. In 1954 the first 120,000 exiles were released, including nearly 25,000 remaining "kulaks" exiled in the 1930s. At the beginning of 1955, passports were issued to all exiles, and although this did not entirely clarify their legal status, it was a harbinger of bigger changes to come. From December 1955 through July 1956, each exiled nationality, including Balkars, Chechens, Crimean Tatars, Ingush, Kalmyks, Karachai, Koreans, Kurds, Meshkhetian Turks, and Soviet Germans, was released from exile as a group. Exiles from Estonia, Latvia, and Lithuania were given permission to return home and reunite with their families in their respective republics. In March 1959 the department in charge of administering the exile settlements was closed, marking the effective end of formal exile of class and national groups by the Soviet state. Although the question of returning "national homelands" to many of these groups remained contested for decades, never again would the Soviet state attempt to resettle entire social groups as a form of collective punishment.

Khrushchev also vigorously pursued policies to reduce the size of the prisoner population. Convicted wartime collaborators were amnestied in September 1955, and German and Japanese nationals convicted of war crimes were released in September 1955 and November 1956 respectively. Intent on reducing the number of "counterrevolutionary" prisoners in the camps, the state ordered the review of their cases. Central and regional commissions operated from 1954 to 1956, and these were followed by traveling commissions sent to various camps in 1956. These commissions freed tens of thousands of prisoners and significantly reduced the sentences of many others. Many prisoners were released because their sentences had been reduced because of amnesties, commissions, credit for productive labor, and parole. According to internal Gulag reports, just over 4 million prisoners were released from March 1953 through the beginning of October 1958. By the beginning of the 1960s, the population of the camps and prisons had fallen to less than a quarter of what it had been on the eve of Stalin's death. Now there many fewer "political" inmates in the camps, but also significantly more repeat offenders.

These mass releases were one part of a larger project to reform the Soviet system of incarceration, attempting to eliminate the negative legacies of Stalinist repression while seeking to preserve its basic core as a penal system intended to punish, isolate, and rehabilitate. Aware that the Gulag was unsustainably large, extraordinarily violent, and extremely corrupt, Khrushchev and his inner circle sought to transform it from a broad tool of social engineering and economic exploitation into a much smaller system that emphasized rehabilitation and humaneness. "Socialist legality," one of the main slogans of Khrushchev's reforms, which promoted the protection of rights rather than the punishment of criminals, was emphasized in new thinking about prisons and criminal justice reform. The Gulag was decentralized, with control of camps (now renamed "colonies" to lessen their association with the Stalin era) devolving to the level of republic and region. The Gulag ceased to be a massive economic empire, with most prisoners now contracted out to other economic enterprises. The reforms of the 1950s were capped by Khrushchev's elimination of both the Gulag and the MVD as union-level institutions. Aside from its important symbolism, this action signaled that the Soviet system of incarceration would be much smaller and more decentralized than it had been in the past. While the rhetoric and practices of "humaneness" were rolled back somewhat in subsequent reforms, there is no question that conditions in Soviet places of incarceration remained much better than they had been under Stalin.

The post-Stalin Gulag was considerably smaller than it had been at its height. The population of Soviet places of incarceration fell over the course of the 1950s, hitting an all-time low of just under 550,000 in 1962. However, the trend of shrinking prison populations did not continue. A return to harsher sentencing practices in the 1960s increased the number of prisoners after 1962, and the prisoner population reached 900,000 in 1970. Population growth was largely flat in the 1970s, but it began to increase again in the early 1980s, reaching a peak of nearly 1.6 million in 1985. It declined again in the second half of the 1980s, reaching approximately 800,000 by the time the USSR collapsed at the end of 1991. Despite these fluctuations, the post-Stalin prison system never approached the incarceration rates of the Stalin era. If the rate reached an all-time high of 1,540 per 100,000 in 1950, it reached its lowest point of 252 per 100,000 in 1961—and never exceeded 600 per 100,000 for the remainder of the Soviet era.

During the mass releases of the post-Stalin era, the number of prisoners held for "political" crimes fell precipitously, and it never returned to previous levels. If approximately one-fifth of the inmates in camps had been "politicals" at the time of Stalin's death, by 1960 there were fewer than 10,000 such prisoners in the system, representing less than 2 percent of the total. Stalin's successors repressed "dissidents" in a more targeted fashion, with many alleged political enemies sentenced to involuntary treatment in a growing network of psychiatric hospitals rather than to incarceration in prisons and colonies. By the 1970s, "special psychiatric hospitals" held tens of thousands of patients, those convicted of crimes (political or otherwise) who were determined by forensic psychiatrists to be mentally ill, and therefore not "criminally responsible." While "treatment" in such facilities was often brutal, the overall scale of incarceration of those convicted of "political" offenses remained much lower than it had been before Stalin's death.

Rehabilitation, restitution, and rights

Once released, prisoners and exiles did not necessarily enjoy full civil rights, and many spent months, years, or even decades working to get such rights restored. In Soviet legal practice, "rehabilitation" was the name given to the process of having one's full rights reestablished. Most released prisoners were issued special passports "with a minus," preventing them from living within 101 kilometers of major cities or in border zones. Combined with a registration system designed to severely restrict in-migration to Moscow, other major cities, and border zones, this significantly curtailed their mobility, economic opportunities, and ability to reunite with loved ones. For the considerable number of former prisoners whose home lay outside the Soviet Union, the process was even more complicated, as return required approval of authorities both inside the USSR and in their home country. Only a full rehabilitation could guarantee former prisoners access to economic compensation, a paltry two months' wages, as well as the right to count their time spent in camps and/or exile toward calculations of an old-age or disability pension. Lack of a full rehabilitation also prevented one from joining or rejoining the Communist Party, a significant limitation on social mobility.

The process for receiving full rehabilitation and the criteria used to grant them were opaque and confusing. Some prisoners, particularly those freed by order of judicial commissions, might be granted rehabilitation immediately upon release, but most of those released via amnesty or the expiration of their sentences had to pursue rehabilitation through the Ministry of Justice. The rehabilitation process was highly personalistic and arbitrary, depending greatly on the disposition of the person considering the case. Those with the right connections were far more likely to receive a positive outcome. Moreover, the judicial apparatus struggled to process the sheer volume of appeals for rehabilitation brought by former prisoners.

According to one estimate, by 1964, the end of the Khrushchev era, authorities had managed to review the cases of just under one-third of those convicted of "counterrevolutionary" crimes during the Stalin era. The pace slowed considerably during the Brezhnev era (1964–82), reflecting much less willingness to confront the legacies of Stalinism, before accelerating rapidly under Gorbachev (1985–91) and after the collapse of the Soviet Union. Absent a full rehabilitation, former prisoners faced significant formal discrimination and were essentially second-class citizens. Informal discrimination against former prisoners was also widespread, creating more barriers to the successful reintegration of former prisoners into Soviet society. Many former prisoners, like Konstantin Petrovich Ivanov, an ex-prisoner who attempted to begin a new life for himself in the city of Vorkuta after release from Vorkutlag in 1955, found themselves in a "gray zone between freedom and unfreedom."

Given persistent and pervasive discrimination against former prisoners, some adopted a somewhat counterintuitive strategy: rather than attempt to return to their former homes, they remained in the area where they had been imprisoned or in exile. There were clear advantages to doing this, particularly if the area was remote. Prisoners often had acquired robust social networks in such places, and informal contacts were essential in securing good jobs and housing after release. Indeed, such networks were often much stronger than what remained where they had lived before arrest and exile. Second, the quick departure of large numbers of prisoners and exiles from regions that had relied on the Gulag created a high demand for labor. Although there were many attempts to recruit young people to relocate to these regions, poor living conditions, not to mention a general culture of violence and coercion, meant that there was high turnover among recruits. Thus, there were often many job opportunities for prisoners or exiles who remained. In many former regions of the Gulag, particularly those located in the Far North, the state offered significant financial incentives to compensate for the obvious hardships of living in such places, and so former prisoners might be able to earn salaries that were double those earned elsewhere. Many former prisoners and exiles chose to remain in place after release, and former Gulag towns like Vorkuta became relatively attractive destinations for former prisoners and exiles seeking to transition to civilian life.

For exiles, full rehabilitation meant not just the restoration of one's civil rights, but also the right of movement. For those who had been deported from a national homeland, the right of return was of paramount concern. Because exile generally involved the punishment of multigenerational families, return was also a family matter. For exiles whose entire national group had been deported followed by the administrative elimination of their homeland, return would also require the restoration of such homelands. In the context of the fraught politics of nationality in the post-Stalin Soviet Union, state officials were not eager to upset the status quo and risk inflaming interethnic conflict, particularly among those who had moved into areas from which national groups had been ethnically cleansed. Only two of the "punished peoples," the Balkars and Karachai, had their homelands completely restored to their pre-deportation status, with pre-existing borders and full-fledged "autonomous region" status within the Russian Federation. The rate of return among these groups appears to have been highest, with more than 80 percent of the registered members of these nationalities living in their national homelands by 1959. The Chechens, Ingushetians, and

Kalmyks returned to territories that excluded key parts of their prewar borders, significantly slowing the rate of return. By 1970, 80 percent of registered Chechens and Kalmyks lived within the borders of their designated homelands, although the rate was significantly lower for Ingushetians. Volga Germans, Crimean Tatars, and Meskhetian Turks never had their homelands restored within the Soviet Union despite collective efforts and international pressure on Soviet leaders. Although many Crimean Tatars did eventually return to Crimea, restitution claims remained a major international issue both in independent Ukraine after 1991 and after the territory was invaded and annexed by Russia in 2014.

Reckoning with the Gulag

The end of mass repression in the Soviet Union, along with the rapid release of millions of prisoners and exiles, was not accompanied by a full public reckoning with the Gulag. The system had been shrouded in secrecy during Stalin's lifetime, and his successors believed that an open discussion of mass repression could destabilize the Soviet system and the legitimacy of its new leaders, who had all been active participants in the machinery of terror. Nikita Khrushchev, the leader who prevailed in the struggle to succeed Stalin, nevertheless made significant efforts to confront the legacies of the Gulag. Khrushchev led two waves of limited public criticism of Stalin's crimes during his so-called "secret speech" at the 20th Party Congress in 1956 and again at the 22nd Party Congress in 1961. Khrushchev was sharply critical of the "cult of personality" that had elevated Stalin to god-like status, and he discussed the repression of political elites during the Great Terror of 1937–38 and after the Second World War. However, such criticism was limited: it did not address widespread repression against ordinary Soviet citizens, nor did it discuss the key role that the Gulag played in the Stalin Revolution.

Khrushchev's "Secret Speech"

Nikita Khrushchev's speech, "On the Cult of Personality," delivered to a closed session of the 20th Congress of the Communist Party of the USSR in February 1956, was a watershed moment in the struggle to come to terms with Stalin's legacy. Over the objections of his closest advisors, he gave a four-hour address that was deeply critical of his predecessor. The core of the speech attacked Stalin's leadership practices and called for a return to the norms of "Leninism" and "socialist legality," but Khrushchev also delivered a series of stunning revelations about the use of terror. Drawing on materials from the re-examination of criminal cases lodged against top state and party leaders, Khrushchev revealed that many of those who had been arrested and executed were innocent and had confessed because of brutal torture by the secret police.

Khrushchev's speech was nevertheless somewhat circumspect in its criticism. He still hailed collectivization and industrialization, extraordinarily violent processes, as great achievements of the Revolution. And while Khrushchev exposed the cruel persecution of loyal elites, the use of terror against Stalin's genuine political enemies, such as Trotsky, remained unquestioned. Most importantly, the speech did not address mass terror against the millions of ordinary Soviet citizens sent into exile or imprisoned in camps. Yet the speech was seen as a signal that a greater public reckoning with the crimes of Stalinism might be possible.

Although it is usually referred to as the "secret speech" because it was delivered at a closed session, the speech's contents were hardly secret at all. A published version was broadly circulated among Communist Party members throughout the USSR, and it was widely leaked—in June 1956, the *New York Times* published a complete translation of the text. It thus ignited international debate about the legacies of Stalinism and the future of the Soviet Union.

Khrushchev's revelations, which eventually reached an audience of millions of Communist Party members throughout the Soviet Union, led to some public reckoning with Stalinist terror and the Gulag. Circumspect discussion of Stalinist terror in Soviet literature began with the publication of Vladimir Dudintsev's novel *Not by Bread Alone* in the journal *Novyi Mir* in August 1956. But it was Aleksandr Solzhenitsyn's 1962 novella *One Day in the Life of Ivan Denisovich* that opened a brief window of public discussion of the Gulag. Personally approved for publication by Khrushchev, it described a day in the life of an ordinary prisoner in a postwar camp. The story was a national and international sensation, inspiring widespread discussions and thousands of letters to the author and the journal in which it appeared. A Gulag survivor himself, Solzhenitsyn depicted the camps through the eyes of an ordinary prisoner, a former peasant. Although it showed neither starvation nor outright brutality, the story conveyed a picture of the camps that was instantly recognized as "authentic" by other survivors, particularly in how it used the criminal argot of the Gulag. *Ivan Denisovich* was followed by the publication of several other literary works that discussed life in the Gulag in Soviet journals, though none approached this work in terms of both literary value and "authenticity." Following Khrushchev's ouster from power, however, public discussions of the Gulag disappeared, as Brezhnev believed that open discussions of Stalinist terror and the Gulag destabilized the Soviet system. Although many survivors and family members of those who had suffered still wanted to discuss their experiences and to see them depicted in literature, there were precious few opportunities to do so until the 1980s.

Literary works examining the Gulag experience did not disappear, however—instead, they went underground. Gulag literature was distributed using two important practices of the late Soviet era: *samizdat* (literally, self-publishing) and *tamizdat* (literally publishing "there," as in abroad). *Samizdat* involved the unofficial circulation of literary works in manuscript form, with duplication performed by an informal network of typists. *Tamizdat*, on the other hand, involved the smuggling of manuscripts outside the country for publication. Solzhenitsyn, whose *Ivan Denisovich* had catapulted him to international literary celebrity, had many of his works published via these methods, including his landmark *Gulag Archipelago*, a massive synthetic history of the Gulag based on the experiences of hundreds of Gulag survivors.

Other key works of underground Gulag literature include Evgeniia Ginzburg's *Krutoi Marshrut* (*Into the Whirlwind*), a memoir of arrest, imprisonment, camp, and life in exile, and Varlam Shalamov's *Kolyma Stories*, a cycle of short stories that remain one of the most harrowing depictions of life in the camps. Aside from works that attained a national and international reputation, many survivors sought to reflect on their experiences in a variety of ways that included not just literary efforts but also oral storytelling, letters, visual art, and drama. This archive of Gulag experience was often hidden in regional museums and personal collections. Comparatively speaking, much less was written about the exile experience, largely because fewer members of these groups belonged to the Soviet intelligentsia. Notably, however, narratives of deportation and exile became an important part of underground political movements for the return of "homelands" to exiled peoples such as the Crimean Tatars. Here, the human rights concerns of the Soviet dissident movement intersected with activism by Gulag survivors and their descendants, with the network of dissident activists and publications supporting the cause of former exiles.

The relaxation of official censorship and spirit of reform that marked the era of *glasnost'* ("openness") under Mikhail Gorbachev in the second half of the 1980s brought much of this "unofficial" Gulag literature and art into the public realm once again. This included not only the official publication of works by Ginzburg, Shalamov, and Solzhenitsyn, but also of new voices on the Gulag experience, such as those contained within *Til My Tale Is Told* (*Dodnes' Tiagoteet*, 1989), a collection of memoirs by women who

9. Former prisoners Evgeniia Ginzburg and Anton Valter with Ginzburg's children, Vasilii Aksenov and Antonina Axenova, in Magadan, Kolyma, in 1949. Ginzburg and Valter lived as exiles in Kolyma until she was "rehabilitated" in 1955. Ginzburg subsequently wrote *Into the Whirlwind*, one of the earliest and most influential Gulag memoirs to be published in the West.

had survived the camps, edited by camp survivor Semien Vilenskii. Nascent civil society also mobilized to advance public reckoning with the legacies of terror and the Gulag, and nongovernmental organizations (NGOs) like Memorial included such efforts within a broader program of democratizing Soviet society. At the same time, some of the first official works that addressed the memory of mass deportations appeared, such as "And the Past Seems but a Dream" (*A proshloe kazhetsia snom*), a 1988 documentary film by Sergei Miroshnichenko that followed the journey of a group of former exiles up the Ensisei River to their former place of exile in Igarka.

Gulag memory after 1991

Although the collapse of the Soviet Union in 1991 seemed to promise that barriers to a full reckoning with the Gulag and its legacy had disappeared, it led to new controversies and conflicts over the place of the Gulag in the history of Russia and the other newly independent states of the former Soviet Union. Whereas before the Soviet collapse the goals of the individuals and organizations pushing for the study and memorialization the Gulag had seemed relatively straightforward, after 1991 the politics of memory of the Gulag became entangled with conflicts about the legacies of the USSR, in particular questions about victimhood, perpetrators, empire, and national independence. What began as a fluid landscape in the late 1980s has since become far more regimented and institutionalized, particularly as state actors have become more actively involved in trying to shape popular memory.

In Russia, there has been an ongoing conflict since the 1990s over how the Gulag should be remembered and who should have control of memorial sites. Stated crudely, the conflict has pitted the Russian state against activists from NGOs, in particular Memorial, a network of organizations dedicated to promoting human rights in the former Soviet Union. State actors seek to limit discussion of the Gulag and avoid linking it to parts of the Soviet legacy that are essential for Russia's post-Soviet identity, particularly victory in World War II and the transformation of the USSR into a global superpower. NGO activists, on the other hand, seek a broader and deeper reckoning with the terror and repression practiced by the Soviet state while emphasizing its linkages to authoritarianism in post-Soviet Russia. While Memorial and other NGOs have remained vital and active, they have been subjected to sustained disruption and harassment by state actors, including classification as "foreign agents" under Russian law, a status that means regular payment of state fines—and in 2022, Memorial was declared illegal in a case argued in front of the Russian Supreme Court. The Russian Orthodox Church figures in this conflict as well. Not only did the clergy face repression in the Soviet era, but many of its properties were used as sites of incarceration and mass executions. Although the church is in many respects an arm of the post-Soviet Russian state, it has its own agenda in memory politics and seeks to use its understanding of Soviet repression to cement its place in the post-Soviet Russian nation.

Conflicts between the state and nonstate activists have played out in a wide range of spaces across Russia, both in major cities and in former outposts of the Gulag, which are often remote. In central Moscow, for example, there are two major Gulag monuments that present sharp contrasts. The first is the so-called Solovetsky Stone, a memory marker from the Solovetsky Islands (home to one of the most important early Soviet prison camps) placed in Moscow in October 1990 in front of Lubianka, the Soviet secret police headquarters. The granite stone, one of five that have been placed in various spaces in Russia, is minimalist in style, with an inscription on the top of the base explaining that it was brought from the Solovetsky camp by the Memorial society and "installed in the memory of the millions of victims of the totalitarian regime." By contrast the "Wall of Sorrow," a 2017 state monument, is massive, featuring a curved wall 100 feet long and 20 feet high, depicting human figures. Both President Putin and Patriarch Kirill, head of the Russian Orthodox church, attended its dedication.

As rival sites of memory, the Solovetsky Stone and Wall of Sorrow even host competing memorial events. Beginning in 2007, Memorial hosted a ceremonial reading of the names of victims of terror on October 29 ("the return of names"), the day *before* the official "Day of Remembrance of the Victims of Political Repressions." Since 2018 the Wall of Sorrow has hosted its own ceremony on October 30, the "Bell of Memory," which offers an opportunity for participants to bring flowers, light a candle, and ring the memorial's "bell," a hanging piece of railroad tie from Solovki. Such a "bell" was typically used in the camps to signify

10. The Solovetsky Stone, the first major memorial to the Gulag and mass terror in the Soviet Union. Placed in October 1990 in front of the KGB headquarters in Moscow, it bears the simple inscription "installed in the memory of the millions of victims of the totalitarian regime."

reveille. While the events do not directly overlap, the contrast between them could not be starker. One is organized by an NGO, where the other is promoted by the state. One is entirely secular, and the other has obvious Christian overtones. The first event focuses on the victims of terror and the crimes committed by the state, whereas the second invokes a more general emotion of grief without attaching it to any particular set of victims or state action.

As a rule, Russian museums have struggled to incorporate the history of the Gulag into their exhibitions. Despite the ubiquity of camps and exile settlements, the majority of regional and local history (*kraevedcheskii*) museums do not mention the Gulag. The minority of museums that do include material on imprisonment or exile often update an existing exhibit on Soviet industrial development or World War II to include a room, corner, or panel describing Gulag activities, displaying archival documents, small objects from the camps, and photographs of both prisoners and camp officials. By including Gulag material within these exhibits, the displays contribute to a narrative that the Gulag was "necessary" to secure the achievements of the Soviet state. Such exhibits rarely tie local camps and exile settlements to the overall Soviet repressive apparatus. Thus, the effect is to remind the visitor that forced labor played a necessary, if unfortunate, role in the industrial development of the region without reflecting on either the overall scale or the broader implications of the Gulag.

A notable exception to this Russian pattern is the Museum of Gulag History in Moscow, which aims to occupy the space of a national museum on the Gulag. Initially a small and eclectic museum run by Gulag survivor Anton Antonov-Ovseenko, it relaunched in October 2015 under the leadership of Roman Romanov, a director with a background in theater and museum studies. Housed in a completely renovated four-story structure, the museum has been internationally recognized for its cutting-edge use of technology and the latest innovations in museum studies. Rather than serving simply as an exhibition space, it plays a broader role for Moscow and Russia as a whole. It works actively with former Gulag victims and their families, serving as a hub for social support and helping families find archival information on repressed relatives. The museum collects testimonies, largely in video form, as part of the "My Gulag" series. It coordinates with regional museums for expeditions to former camp sites and for traveling exhibitions. Like the 2017 Wall of Sorrow monument, it can be seen as an attempt by the Russian state to keep Gulag memorialization under the control of state organizations rather than in the hands of NGOs like Memorial with close ties to the international human rights movement. Although the museum tells a coherent narrative of the Gulag, questions about victims and perpetrators, as well as the overall place of the Gulag within the broader Soviet project, remain largely unexplored.

Museums outside Russia, not surprisingly, emphasize national victimhood at the hands of occupying Russian (and Soviet) forces, even as they vary in their approach to memory. In the Baltic states of Estonia, Latvia, and Lithuania, where Soviet rule is treated as a foreign occupation, museums and memorials are unambiguous in their depiction of the Gulag. For example, the Museum of Occupations and Freedom Fights in Lithuania, located in Vilnius, examines the forced deportation and incarceration of Lithuanians in the Gulag as part of a narrative of Soviet genocide directed against Lithuanian people. Museum exhibits affirm the sovereignty of post-Soviet Lithuania through the depiction of Lithuanian victimhood at the hands of Soviet perpetrators. Although the museum has been criticized for ignoring Lithuanian collaboration with Soviet occupiers, for seeming to equate Soviet terror with the Holocaust, and for overlooking the plight of non-Lithuanian victims of Soviet Terror (such as Roma and Jews), the Museum of Occupations offers an unambiguous moral perspective on the Gulag. In Kazakhstan, memorial museums near the cities of Astana and Karaganda depict the Gulag as a series of crimes perpetrated by Russians against Kazakhs without interrogating a complex historical situation: on one hand, many of the victims in these camps were not Kazakhs; on the other, many Kazakhs served as eager perpetrators. The situation is also complicated by the fact that Kazakhstan's post-Soviet ruling elite is largely a continuation of what existed in the late Soviet era. Thus, although museums and memorials of the Gulag outside Russia try to draw clear lines between perpetrator and victim that match up with colonizer and colonized, they run the risk of oversimplifying the complex effects and legacies of the Gulag in non-Russian parts of the Soviet Union.

Prisons and camps after 1991: a neo-Gulag?

The Soviet collapse held out great promise for reforming criminal justice and places of incarceration across the former Soviet Union, and in particular, for dispensing with many of the most problematic legacies that remained from the Stalin era. These legacies included high rates of incarceration, the persistence of criminal groupings and violence, and general lack of resources and staffing. Overall, the 1990s saw little headway in these areas in most of the Soviet successor states, as economic collapse, widespread corruption, and weakening state capacities drove up crime and incarceration rates. By 2000, Russia reached an incarceration rate of 729 per 100,000, the highest rate of incarceration seen since the post-Stalin reforms of the middle of the 1950s. Most other Soviet successor states also experienced significant increases.

Since 2000 most post-Soviet states have experienced the opposite trend, with incarceration rates falling significantly. As of 2020, Russia's rate fell to 323 per 100,000—one of the lowest years on record since the early 1930s—though it still represents one of the highest rates of incarceration in the world. Reforms to the internal operations of prison systems have seen much less success, however. In Russia, "collectivist" living in barracks, prisoner self-governance, and mutual policing and informants remain central to the day-to-day operation of penal institutions. In such conditions, criminal groupings have remained powerful, with a "reputation system" of argot, tattoos, and violence continuing to regulate relations among prisoners. Although the economic importance of unfree labor has continued to diminish in post-Soviet Russia, some regions and localities still specialize in penal institutions and holding prisoners—a clear legacy of Stalinism. Stiffening the punishment of prisoners by sending them to isolated places of incarceration that are far from their homes is a practice that also continues in Russia. Other post-Soviet states, such as Kyrgyzstan, Moldova, and Uzbekistan, have generally followed the Russian model, reducing their rates of incarceration without any fundamental reforms of internal prison dynamics.

Estonia, Georgia, Kazakhstan, Latvia, and Lithuania have attempted more thoroughgoing reforms of their systems of incarceration. In particular, they seek to reject the Soviet legacy of "collectivist" living, moving instead to prison designs that are based around individual cells. In such a system, surveillance of prisoner behavior is carried out by guards rather than mutual surveillance and informants. Prison architecture, official skepticism, and long-standing prisoner practices have created barriers to such reforms. However, all of these countries have claimed significant progress in improving conditions and reducing violence between prisoners. Overall, although post-Soviet states have pursued different paths in reforming their systems of criminal justice and incarceration, all continue to struggle with the legacies of the Gulag to a greater or lesser degree.

Legacies and perspectives

Many legacies of the Stalinist Gulag remain in the countries that were once part of the Soviet Union. This is perhaps most apparent in the areas that housed the largest number of camps and places of exile, particularly Russia and Kazakhstan, where patterns of settlement and economic structures were profoundly shaped by unfree labor. Yet because the system's victims came from many different locations, population categories, and demographics, the Gulag's legacies continue to be widespread—and since the Gulag held millions of noncitizens, particularly during and after World War II, this extends beyond the borders of the former USSR. Although few people with direct experiences and memories of the Gulag linger among the living, second- and third-generation traumas remain within families and social networks. Conflicts over memory, memorialization, and, ultimately, what lessons can be gleaned from this collective trauma have not abated. Why else would the Russian state have taken the extraordinary step of launching a judicial process to shut down the country's largest NGO dedicated to the memory of Stalinist terror, Memorial, nearly seventy years after Stalin's death? When considering history and memory, no issues can ever be considered settled—but the Russian state's recent efforts to clamp down on Memorial and other NGOs suggest that understandings of the Gulag and its place in the histories of post-Soviet states remain divisive—and relevant.

Coming to terms with the significance and legacies of the Stalinist Gulag means rethinking its place in global histories of topics that include the modern prison and penal policy, forced labor, and the concentration camp. The Gulag was a distinctly Soviet institution that nevertheless shared characteristics with other modern systems of mass punishment. It was distinguished first and foremost by its scale. Whether in terms of the number of victims, rates of incarceration, or geographic spread, the Gulag was one of the largest penal systems in modern history. It was, like other modern systems of forced labor and exile, a place of mass death. Although it is difficult to calculate death rates with certainty, best estimates suggest that more than about one out of every five prisoners and exiles perished between 1930 and 1960, making it one of the deadliest penal systems in modern history.

The Gulag was also a system of mass incarceration, with Soviet citizens sentenced to imprisonment or exile at some of the highest rates of any other modern society. This reflected the Stalinist polity, which criminalized a wide range of behaviors and punished them harshly. The Gulag was distinguished by its overwhelming emphasis on forced labor—the notion that prisoners and exiles constituted a cheap and mobile labor source profoundly shaped policies and practices in the Gulag—and the development of the Soviet system in general. The centrality of the Gulag to the Stalinist project made it a key part of the experience of millions of Soviet citizens, and rendered its histories and legacies high stakes exercises both immediately after Stalin's death and after the collapse of the USSR.

References

Chapter 1

Aleksandr Solzhenitsyn, *The Gulag Archipelago, 1918–1956*, trans. Thomas P. Whitney (New York: Harper and Row, 1974), 2:7.

"In exile imprisonment": Laura Piacentini and Judith Pallot, "'In Exile Imprisonment' in Russia," *British Journal of Criminology* 54, no. 1 (January 1, 2014): 20–37.

Mass imprisonment: David Garland, "Introduction: The Meaning of Mass Imprisonment," *Punishment & Society* 3, no. 1 (January 1, 2001): 5–6.

Rates of incarceration in the United States: "United States of America," *World Prison Brief*, accessed April 5, 2022, https://www.prisonstudies.org/country/united-states-america.

Panopticon: Michel Foucault, *Discipline and Punish: The Birth of the Prison*, trans. Alan Sheridan (New York: Pantheon Books, 1977), chap. 3.

Polyopticon: Laura Piacentini and Gavin Slade, "Architecture and Attachment: Carceral Collectivism and the Problem of Prison Reform in Russia and Georgia," *Theoretical Criminology* 19, no. 2 (2015): 182.

"State of exception": Giorgio Agamben, *Homo Sacer: Sovereign Power and Bare Life* (Stanford, CA: Stanford University Press, 1998), 9.

Margarete Buber-Neumann, *Under Two Dictators: Prisoner of Stalin and Hitler*, trans. Edward Fitzgerald (London: Pimlico, 2008), 163, 193.

Chapter 2

Number of prisoners in 1914: Michael Jakobson, *Origins of the Gulag: The Soviet Prison Camp System, 1917–1934* (Lexington: University Press of Kentucky, 1993), 10–11.

Number of exiles in 1898: Sarah Badcock, *A Prison Without Walls? Eastern Siberian Exile in the Last Years of Tsarism* (Oxford: Oxford University Press, 2016), 14.

"Concentration camps": S. A. Krasil'nikov, "Rozhdenie GULAGa: diskussii v verknykh eshelonakh vlasti," *Istoricheskii arkhiv*, no. 4 (1997): 143–44, 152.

Crime in 1927 and 1933: Oleg Mozokhin, *Statisticheskie svedeniia o deiatel'nosti organov VChK-OGPU-NKVD-MGB (1918–1953 gg.): statisticheskii spravochnik* (Moscow: Algoritm, 2016).

Number of prisoners in 1936: O. V. Khlevniuk, *The History of the Gulag: From Collectivization to the Great Terror*, trans. Vadim Staklo (New Haven, CT: Yale University Press, 2004), 30–31, 167–68.

Eugenia Ginzburg, *Journey into the Whirlwind*, trans. Paul Stevenson and Max Hayward (New York: Harvest/HBJ Books, 2002), 270.

BAMlag in 1938: A. B. Bezborodov and V. M. Khrustalev, eds., *Naselenie Gulaga: chislennost' i usloviia soderzhaniia*, vol. 4, Istoriia stalinskogo Gulaga: konets 1920-kh—pervaia polovina 1950-kh: sobranie dokumentov v semi tomakh (Moscow: ROSSPEN, 2004), 158–59.

Total victims from Order no. 00447 and on new logging camps: O. V. Khlevniuk, *The History of the Gulag: From Collectivization to the Great Terror*, trans. Vadim Staklo (New Haven: Yale University Press, 2004), 177–78.

Executions in Ukhtpechlag: M. B. Rogachev, "'Operatsiia po prikazu 00409' v Ukhto-Pechorskom ITL," in *Pokaiane: Komi republikan-skii martirolog zhertv massovykh politicheskykh represseii*, vol. 8 pt. 2, ed. E. A. Zelenskaia and M. B. Rogachev (Syktyvkar: Pokaianie, 2006), 181–209.

On the deportation of Finns and Koreans: V. N. Zemskov, *Spetsposelentsy v SSSR, 1930–1960* (Moscow: Nauka, 2003), 78–81.

Number of people deported from western borderlands: Pavel Polian, *Against Their Will: The History and Geography of Forced Migrations in the USSR* (New York: Central European University Press, 2003), 123, 157.

Total exiles at the end of World War II: T. V. Tsarevskskaia-Diakina, ed., *Spetspereselentsy v SSSR*, vol. 5, Istoriia stalinskogo Gulaga: konets 1920-kh—pervaia polovina 1950-kh: sobranie dokumentov v semi tomakh (Moscow: ROSSPEN, 2004), 69.

Prisoners conscripted, 1941–45: Iurii Aleksandrovich Poliakov, *Naselenie Rossii v XX veke: istoricheskie ocherki*, vol. 2, 1940–59 (Moscow: ROSSPEN, 2001), 184.

Number of "mobilized" Soviet Germans: V. N. Zemskov, *Spetsposelentsy v SSSR, 1930–1960* (Moscow: Nauka, 2003), 94–95.

Released prisoners held in camps until the end of World War II: A. B. Bezborodov and V. M. Khrustalev, eds., *Naselenie Gulaga: chislennost' i usloviia soderzhaniia*, vol. 4, Istoriia stalinskogo Gulaga: konets 1920-kh—pervaia polovina 1950-kh: sobranie dokumentov v semi tomakh (Moscow: ROSSPEN, 2004), 102–103.

"Betrayers of the motherland, spies or saboteurs": N. V. Petrov, ed., *Karatel'naia sistema: struktura i kadry*, vol. 2, Istoriia stalinskogo Gulaga: konets 1920-kh—pervaia polovina 1950-kh: sobranie dokumentov v semi tomakh (Moscow: ROSSPEN, 2004), 211–13.

Former POWs and Soviet citizens who had lived in occupation subject to forced labor: State Archive of the Russian Federation (GARF) fond (f.) R-9414, opis' (op.) 1, delo (d.) 1230, list (l.) 36.

1945 amnesty: Golfo Alexopoulos, "Amnesty 1945: The Revolving Door of Stalin's Gulag," *Slavic Review* 64, no. 2 (2005): 274–306.

Number of POWs: Maksim Matveevich Zagorul'ko, ed., *Voennoplennye v SSSR 1939–1956: dokumenty i materialy* (Moscow: Logos, 2000), 1038.

Theft convictions, 1946–59: S. V. Mironenko and N. Werth, eds., *Massovye repressii v SSSR*, vol. 1, Istoriia stalinskogo Gulaga: konets 1920-kh—pervaia polovina 1950-kh: sobranie dokumentov v semi tomakh (Moscow: ROSSPEN, 2004), 564.

Proportion of prisoners in the Gulag with theft convictions: Juliette Cadiot, *La société des voleurs: propriété et socialisme sous Staline* (Paris: Editions EHESS, 2021), 246.

Sentences after the war: A. B. Bezborodov and V. M. Khrustalev, eds., *Naselenie Gulaga: chislennost' i usloviia soderzhaniia*, vol. 4, Istoriia stalinskogo Gulaga: konets 1920-kh—pervaia polovina 1950-kh: sobranie dokumentov v semi tomakh (Moscow: ROSSPEN, 2004), 117, 120, 129.

Georgii Demidov, "No Toe Tag," trans. Brian Kilgour et al., in *Five Fates from a Wonderous Planet*, ed. Diane Nemec Ignashev (Moscow: Vozvrashchenie, 2015), 67–68.

Special camp prisoner numbers: A. B. Roginskii, M. B. Smirnov, and N. G. Okhotin, *Sistema ispravitel'no-trudovykh lagerei v SSSR, 1923-1960: Spravochnik* (Moscow: Zven'ia, 1998), 52–53.

Number of postwar exiles and escape from exile: T. V. Tsarevskskaia-Diakina, ed., *Spetspereselentsy v SSSR*, vol. 5, Istoriia stalinskogo Gulaga: konets 1920-kh—pervaia polovina 1950-kh: sobranie dokumentov v semi tomakh (Moscow: ROSSPEN, 2004), 72–79.

Chapter 3

Convictions under antitheft laws: A. B. Bezborodov and V. M. Khrustalev, eds., *Naselenie Gulaga: chislennost' i usloviia soderzhaniia*, vol. 4, Istoriia stalinskogo Gulaga: konets 1920-kh—pervaia polovina 1950-kh: sobranie dokumentov v semi tomakh (Moscow: ROSSPEN, 2004), 39.

Proportion of prisoners convicted of "counter-revolutionary crimes": J. Arch Getty, Gábor T. Rittersporn, and Viktor N. Zemskov, "Victims of the Soviet Penal System in the Pre-War Years: A First Approach on the Basis of Archival Evidence," *American Historical Review* 98, no. 4 (October 1993): 1048–49.

Balashina: Jehanne M. Gheith and Katherine R. Jolluck, eds., *Gulag Voices: Oral Histories of Soviet Incarceration and Exile* (New York: Palgrave Macmillan, 2011), chap. 1.

Proportion of prisoners aged 25 to 40: J. Arch Getty, Gábor T. Rittersporn, and Viktor N. Zemskov, "Victims of the Soviet Penal System in the Pre-War Years: A First Approach on the Basis of Archival Evidence," *American Historical Review* 98, no. 4 (October 1993): 1025.

"The Artist Bacillus and his Masterpiece": Georgii Demidov, *Five Fates from a Wondrous Planet*, ed. and trans. Diane Nemec Ignashev (Moscow: Vozvrashchenie, 2015), 168–93.

Labor colonies for juveniles: A. B. Bezborodov and V. M. Khrustalev, eds., *Naselenie Gulaga: chislennost' i usloviia soderzhaniia*, vol. 4, Istoriia stalinskogo Gulaga: konets 1920-kh—pervaia polovina 1950-kh: sobranie dokumentov v semi tomakh (Moscow: ROSSPEN, 2004), 81–84.

Absolute number of women in camps: J. Arch Getty, Gábor T. Rittersporn, and Viktor N. Zemskov, "Victims of the Soviet Penal System in the Pre-War Years: A First Approach on the Basis of Archival Evidence," *American Historical Review* 98, no. 4 (October 1993): 1025.

Relative number of women in camps: Golfo Alexopoulos, "Exiting the Gulag after the War: Women, Invalids, and the Family," *Jahrbücher für Geschichte Osteuropas* 57, no. 4 (2009): 568.

Memoirs of Maria L'vovna Danilenko: M. L. Danilenko. "Steregli nas kak zoloto, a tsenili kak g…", in *Stranitsy tragicheskikh sudeb: Sb. Vospominanii zhertv polit. repressii v SSSR v 1920-1950-e gg.*, ed. E. M. Gribanova et al. (Almaty: Zheti zhagry, 2002), 82.

Infant mortality: Donald A. Filtzer, *The Hazards of Urban Life in Late Stalinist Russia: Health, Hygiene, and Living Standards, 1943-1953* (Cambridge: Cambridge University Press, 2010), 258.

Tamara Petkevich, *Memoir of a Gulag Actress*, trans., Yasha Klots and Ross Ufberg (Ithaca, NY: Cornell University Press, 2010), 173–74, 200–203.

Nationality of prisoners in Vorkuta camps: Alan Barenberg, *Gulag Town, Company Town: Forced Labor and Its Legacy in Vorkuta* (New Haven, CT: Yale University Press, 2014), 101.

Foreign prisoners in the Gulag in 1939: A. B. Bezborodov and V. M. Khrustalev, eds., *Naselenie Gulaga: chislennost' i usloviia soderzhaniia*, vol. 4, Istoriia stalinskogo Gulaga: konets 1920-kh—pervaia polovina 1950-kh: sobranie dokumentov v semi tomakh (Moscow: ROSSPEN, 2004), 75–76.

Central Gulag employees, 1930 to 1939: G. M. Ivanova, *Labor Camp Socialism: The Gulag in the Soviet Totalitarian System*, trans. Carol Flath (Armonk, NY: M. E. Sharpe, 2000), 143.

Vacancies in 1947: N. V. Petrov, ed., *Karatel'naia sistema: struktura i kadry*, vol. 2, Istoriia stalinskogo Gulaga: konets 1920-kh—pervaia polovina 1950-kh: sobranie dokumentov v semi tomakh (Moscow: ROSSPEN, 2004), 355–57.

Ivan Chistyakov, *The Day Will Pass Away: The Diary of a Gulag Prison Guard, 1935-1936*, trans. A. L. Tait (New York: Pegasus Books, 2017).

Fyodor Vasilevich Mochulsky, *Gulag Boss: A Soviet Memoir*, trans. Deborah Kaple (New York: Oxford University Press, 2010), 32–34.

Chapter 4

Evfrosiniia Kersnovskaia, *Skol'ko stoit chelovek* (Moscow: KoLibri, 2016), 530.

"Nutritional dystrophy": Rebecca Manley, "Nutritional Dystrophy: The Science and Semantics of Starvation in World War II," in *Hunger and War: Food Provisioning in the Soviet Union during World*

War II, ed. Wendy Z. Goldman and Donald A. Filtzer (Bloomington: Indiana University Press, 2015), 206–64.

"Shock Therapy": Varlam Shalamov, *Kolyma Stories*, trans. Donald Rayfield (New York: NYRB Classics, 2018), 157–66. Quotation from 158.

Kuskov letter: Elena Zhemkova et al., *Pravo perepiski*, 2nd ed. (Moscow: Agei Tomesh, 2017), 122.

Hospital beds: Dan Healey, "Lives in the Balance: Weak and Disabled Prisoners and the Biopolitics of the Gulag," *Kritika: Explorations in Russian and Eurasian History* 16, no. 3 (2015): 528–29.

1944 health regulations: A. B. Bezborodov and V. M. Khrustalev, eds., *Naselenie Gulaga: chislennost' i usloviia soderzhaniia*, vol. 4, Istoriia stalinskogo Gulaga: konets 1920-kh—pervaia polovina 1950-kh: sobranie dokumentov v semi tomakh (Moscow: ROSSPEN, 2004), 517.

"Dominoes": Varlam Shalamov, *Kolyma Stories*, trans. Donald Rayfield (New York: NYRB Classics, 2018), 143–52.

USSR mortality figures: Iurii Aleksandrovich Poliakov, *Naselenie Rossii v XX veke: istoricheskie ocherki*, vol. 1, 1900–39 (Moscow: ROSSPEN, 2000), 267–68, 340.

Gulag mortality figures: A. B. Bezborodov and V. M. Khrustalev, eds., *Naselenie Gulaga: chislennost' i usloviia soderzhaniia*, vol. 4, Istoriia stalinskogo Gulaga: konets 1920-kh—pervaia polovina 1950-kh: sobranie dokumentov v semi tomakh (Moscow: ROSSPEN, 2004), 55; V. N. Zemskov, *Spetsposelentsy v SSSR, 1930–1960* (Moscow: Nauka, 2003), 20.

Moscow mortality figures: Donald A. Filtzer, *The Hazards of Urban Life in Late Stalinist Russia: Health, Hygiene, and Living Standards, 1943–1953* (Cambridge: Cambridge University Press, 2010), 176.

"Special Settlements" mortality in 1930: Lynne Viola, *The Unknown Gulag: The Lost World of Stalin's Special Settlements* (New York: Oxford University Press, 2007), 114.

Mortality among Chechen, German, Ingush exiles: V. N. Zemskov, *Spetsposelentsy v SSSR, 1930–1960* (Moscow: Nauka, 2003), 281.

"Nazino Affair" deaths: Nicolas Werth, *Cannibal Island: Death in a Siberian Gulag* (Princeton, NJ: Princeton University Press, 2007).

Mortality in Vorkuta: Alan Barenberg, *Gulag Town, Company Town: Forced Labor and Its Legacy in Vorkuta* (New Haven: Yale University Press, 2014), 270.

Underreporting of deaths: Mikhail Nakonechnyi, "'Factory of Invalids': Mortality, Disability, and Early Release on Medical

Grounds in GULAG, 1930–1955" (Ph.D., University of Oxford, 2020), 5.

Varlam Shalamov, *Kolyma Stories*, trans. Donald Rayfield (New York: NYRB Classics, 2018), xv.

Chapter 5

Julius Margolin, *Journey into the Land of the Zeks and Back: A Memoir of the Gulag*, trans. Stefani Hoffman (New York: Oxford University Press, 2020), 114.

Prisoners "must cover their own expenses": Pis'mo v TsKK RKP(b) o karatel'noi politike Sovetskogo gosudarstvo 17.02.1924, *Fond Aleksandra N. Iakovleva*, accessed April 7, 2022, https://www.alexanderyakovlev.org/fond/issues-doc/1019829.

"Colonization of uninhabited areas": Pis'mo I. S. Unshlikhtu o printsipakh karatel'noi politiki GPU v mirnoe vremia 16.08.1923, *Fond Aleksandra N. Iakovleva*, accessed April 7, 2022, https://www.alexanderyakovlev.org/fond/issues-doc/1019707.

Ten percent of capital investments: Yoram Gorlizki and O. V. Khlevniuk, *Cold Peace: Stalin and the Soviet Ruling Circle, 1945–1953* (New York: Oxford University Press, 2004), 127.

Number of prisoners working on Belmorkanal: O. V. Khlevniuk, *The History of the Gulag: From Collectivization to the Great Terror*, trans. Vadim Staklo (New Haven, CT: Yale University Press, 2004), 35.

Deaths building Belomorkanal: A. B. Bezborodov and V. M. Khrustalev, eds., *Naselenie Gulaga: chislennost' i usloviia soderzhaniia*, vol. 4, Istoriia stalinskogo Gulaga: konets 1920-kh—pervaia polovina 1950-kh: sobranie dokumentov v semi tomakh (Moscow: ROSSPEN, 2004), 465, 477.

Forestry camps: Paul R. Gregory, "An Introduction to the Economics of the Gulag," in *The Economics of Forced Labor: The Soviet Gulag*, ed. Paul R. Gregory and V. V. Lazarev (Stanford, CA: Hoover Institution Press, 2003), 13.

Contract labor: Wilson T. Bell, *Stalin's Gulag at War* (Toronto: University of Toronto Press, 2018), 155.

John Scott, *Behind the Urals: An American Worker in Russia's City of Steel*. Bloomington: Indiana University Press, 1989.

Proportion of forced laborers in Nazi Germany: Mark Spoerer and Jochen Fleischhacker, "Forced Laborers in Nazi Germany: Categories, Numbers, and Survivors," *Journal of Interdisciplinary History*, no. 2 (2002): 198.

1939 food regulations: A. B. Bezborodov and V. M. Khrustalev, eds., *Naselenie Gulaga: chislennost' i usloviia soderzhaniia*, vol. 4, Istoriia stalinskogo Gulaga: konets 1920-kh—pervaia polovina 1950-kh: sobranie dokumentov v semi tomakh (Moscow: ROSSPEN, 2004), 342–49.

"Typhus Quarantine": Varlam Shalamov, *Kolyma Stories*, trans. Donald Rayfield (New York: NYRB Classics, 2018), 202.

Chapter 6

Release of exiles: T. V. Tsarevskskaia-Diakina, ed., *Spetspereselentsy v SSSR*, vol. 5, Istoriia stalinskogo Gulaga: konets 190-kh—pervaia polovina 1950-kh: sobranie dokumentov v semi tomakh (Moscow: ROSSPEN, 2004), 91–92.

Prisoner releases, 1954 to 1958: GARF f. R-9414, op. 1 ch. 2, d. 519, ll. 124–28.

Prisoner population in 1960: Jeffrey S. Hardy, *The Gulag after Stalin: Redefining Punishment in Khrushchev's Soviet Union, 1953–1964* (Ithaca, NY: Cornell University Press, 2016), 54–57.

"Politicals" in the prisoner population, 1960: Marc Elie, "Khrushchev's Gulag: the Soviet Penitentiary System after Stalin's death, 1953–1964," in *The Thaw: Soviet Society and Culture during the 1950s and 1960s*, ed. Eleonory Gilburd and Denis Kozlov (Toronto: University of Toronto Press, 2013), 113, 119.

Prisoner population 1962 to 1991: Alain Blum, Françoise Daucé, Marc Elie, and Isabelle Ohayon, *L'âge soviétique: une traversée de l'Empire russe au monde postsoviétique* (Paris: Armand Colin, 2021), 165.

Psychiatric hospitals: Garret J. McDonald, "The Delusion of Reform: Soviet Law, Forensic Psychiatry, and the Fate of Dissent after Stalin" (Ph.D., Fordham University, 2023), chap. 5.

Ivanov quoted in: Tyler C. Kirk, "Memory of Vorkuta: A Gulag Returnee's Attempts at Autobiography and Art," *Kritika: Explorations in Russian and Eurasian History* 21, no. 1 (2020): 108.

Rates of return of exiles: Pavel Polian, *Against Their Will: The History and Geography of Forced Migrations in the USSR* (New York: Central European University Press, 2003), 198.

Incarceration rates in Russia: "Russian Federation," *World Prison Brief*, accessed April 5, 2022, https://www.prisonstudies.org/country/russian-federation.

Further reading

General studies and anthologies

Alexopoulos, Golfo. *Illness and Inhumanity in Stalin's Gulag.* New Haven, CT: Yale University Press, 2017.

Applebaum, Anne. *Gulag: A History.* New York: Doubleday, 2003.

Barenberg, Alan. *Gulag Town, Company Town: Forced Labor and Its Legacy in Vorkuta.* New Haven, CT: Yale University Press, 2014.

Barenberg, Alan and Emily D. Johnson, eds. *Rethinking the Gulag: Identities, Sources, Legacies.* Bloomington: Indiana University Press, 2022.

Barnes, Steven A. *Death and Redemption: The Gulag and the Shaping of Soviet Society.* Princeton, NJ: Princeton University Press, 2011.

Bell, Wilson T. *Stalin's Gulag at War.* Toronto: University of Toronto Press, 2018.

David-Fox, Michael, ed. *The Soviet Gulag: Evidence, Interpretation, and Comparison.* Pittsburgh: University of Pittsburgh Press, 2016.

Gregory, Paul R. and V. V. Lazarev, eds. *The Economics of Forced Labor: The Soviet Gulag.* Stanford, CA: Hoover Institution Press, 2003.

Gullotta, Andrea. *Intellectual Life and Literature at Solovki 1923–1930: The Paris of the Northern Concentration Camps.* Oxford: Legenda, Modern Humanities Research Association, 2018.

Khlevniuk, O. V. *The History of the Gulag: From Collectivization to the Great Terror.* Trans. Vadim Staklo. New Haven, CT: Yale University Press, 2004.

Kis, Oksana. *Survival as Victory: Ukrainian Women in the Gulag.* Trans. Lidia Wolanskyj. Cambridge, MA: Harvard University Press, 2020.

Naimark, Norman. *Stalin's Genocides*. Princeton, NJ: Princeton University Press, 2011.

Polian, Pavel. *Against Their Will: The History and Geography of Forced Migrations in the USSR*. New York: Central European University Press, 2003.

Ruder, Cynthia A. *Building Stalinism: The Moscow Canal and the Creation of Soviet Space*. London: Bloomsbury, 2019.

Straw, Andrew Dale. "Resisting Ethnic Cleansing: Crimean Tatars, Crimea, and the Soviet Union, 1941–1991." Ph.D. Dissertation, University of Texas-Austin, 2017.

Toker, Leona. *Return from the Archipelago: Narratives of Gulag Survivors*. Bloomington: Indiana University Press, 2000.

Viola, Lynne. *The Unknown Gulag: The Lost World of Stalin's Special Settlements*. New York: Oxford University Press, 2007.

Westren, Michael Herceg. "Nations in Exile: 'The Punished Peoples' in Soviet Kazakhstan, 1941–1961." Ph.D. Dissertation, University of Chicago, 2012.

Terror, crime, policing

Conquest, Robert. *The Great Terror: A Reassessment*. New York: Oxford University Press, 1990.

Getty, J. Arch and Oleg V. Naumov. *The Road to Terror: Stalin and the Self-Destruction of the Bolsheviks, 1932–1939*. New Haven, CT: Yale University Press, 1999.

Gregory, Paul R. *Terror by Quota: State Security from Lenin to Stalin (An Archival Study)*. New Haven, CT: Yale University Press, 2009.

Hagenloh, Paul. *Stalin's Police: Public Order and Mass Repression in the USSR, 1926–1941*. Baltimore: Johns Hopkins University Press, 2009.

Shearer, David R. *Policing Stalin's Socialism: Repression and Social Order in the Soviet Union, 1924–1953*. New Haven, CT: Yale University Press, 2009.

Vatlin, Alexander. *Agents of Terror: Ordinary Men and Extraordinary Violence in Stalin's Secret Police*. Ed. and trans. Seth Bernstein. Madison: University of Wisconsin Press, 2016.

Viola, Lynne. *Stalinist Perpetrators on Trial: Scenes from the Great Terror in Soviet Ukraine*. New York: Oxford University Press, 2017.

Memoirs and literary works

Adamova-Sliozberg, Ol'ga. *My Journey: How One Woman Survived Stalin's Gulag*. Evanston, IL: Northwestern University Press, 2011.

Applebaum, Anne, ed. *Gulag Voices: An Anthology*. New Haven, CT: Yale University Press, 2011.

Bardach, Janusz and Kathleen Gleeson. *Man Is Wolf to Man: Surviving the Gulag*. Berkeley: University of California Press, 1998.

Bardach, Janusz and Kathleen Gleeson, *Surviving Freedom: After the Gulag*. Berkeley: University of California Press, 2003.

Buber-Neumann, Margarete. *Under Two Dictators: Prisoner of Stalin and Hitler*. Trans. Edward Fitzgerald. London: Pimlico, 2008.

Chistyakov, Ivan. *The Day Will Pass Away: The Diary of a Gulag Prison Guard, 1935–1936*. Trans. A. L. Tait. New York: Pegasus Books, 2017.

Demidov, Georgii. *Five Fates from a Wonderous Planet*. Ed. and trans. Diane Nemec Ignashev. Moscow: Vozvrashchenie, 2015.

Formakov, Arsenii. *Gulag Letters*. Ed. and trans. Emily D. Johnson. New Haven, CT: Yale University Press, 2017.

Ginzburg, Eugenia. *Journey into the Whirlwind*. Trans. Paul Stevenson and Max Hayward. New York: Harvest/HBJ Books, 2002.

Ginzburg, Eugenia. *Within the Whirlwind*. Trans. Ian Boland. New York: Harcourt Brace Jovanovich, 1981.

Mochulsky, Fyodor Vasilevich. *Gulag Boss: A Soviet Memoir*. Trans. Deborah Kaple. New York: Oxford University Press, 2010.

Petkevich, Tamara. *Memoir of a Gulag Actress*. Trans. Yasha Klots and Ross Ufberg. Ithaca, NY: Cornell University Press, 2010.

Shalamov, Varlam. *Kolyma Stories*. Trans. Donald Rayfield. New York: NYRB Classics, 2018.

Shalamov, Varlam. *Sketches of the Criminal World: Further Kolyma Stories*. Trans. Donald Rayfield. New York: NYRB Classics, 2020.

Solzhenitsyn, Aleksandr *The Gulag Archipelago, 1918–1956*. Trans. Thomas P. Whitney. New York: Harper and Row, 1974.

Solzhenitsyn, Aleksandr. *One Day in the Life of Ivan Denisovich*. Trans. Ralph Parker. New York: New American Library, 2009.

Vilensky, Simeon, ed. *Till My Tale Is Told: Women's Memoirs of the Gulag*. Trans. John Crowfoot et al. Bloomington: Indiana University Press, 1999.

Vladimov, Georgii. *Faithful Ruslan*. Trans. Michael Glenny. Brooklyn: Melville House, 2011.

Gulag legacies

Adler, Nanci. *The Gulag Survivor: Beyond the Soviet System*. New Brunswick, NJ: Transaction Publishers, 2002.

Bogumil, Zuzanna. *Gulag Memories: The Rediscovery and Commemoration of Russia's Repressive Past*. Trans. Philip Palmer. New York: Berghahn Books, 2011.

Dobson, Miriam. *Khrushchev's Cold Summer: Gulag Returnees, Crime, and the Fate of Reform after Stalin*. Ithaca, NY: Cornell University Press, 2009.

Gavrilova, Sofia. *Russia's Regional Museums: Representing and Misrepresenting Knowledge about Nature, History and Society*. Milton, UK: Taylor & Francis Group, 2022.

Kirk, Tyler. *After the Gulag: A History of Memory in Russia's Far North*. Bloomington: Indiana University Press, 2023.

Norris, Stephen M., ed. *Museums of Communism: New Memory Sites in Central and Eastern Europe*. Bloomington: Indiana University Press, 2020.

Smith, Kathleen E. *Moscow 1956: The Silenced Spring*. Cambridge, MA: Harvard University Press, 2017.

Websites

European memories of the Gulag

https://museum.gulagmemories.eu/en/
A collection of materials on national deportations and life in exile, featuring testimonies, images, archival materials, and films.

Gulag History Museum

https://gmig.ru/en/
The web site of the State Gulag Museum in Moscow. Includes virtual exhibits, an interactive map, and other materials.

Gulag: Many Days, Many Lives

https://gulaghistory.org/
This is a virtual archive of the Gulag featuring virtual museum exhibitions and an archive.

Gulag Maps

https://www.gulagmaps.org/
A collection of virtual maps and resources created under the auspices of the "Mapping the Gulag" research project.

Memorial Society International

https://www.memo.ru/en-us/
The web site of Russia's largest NGO dedicated to human rights and the memory of Soviet repression, featuring many digital projects. No longer updated as of April 2022.

Moscow-Volga.Ru: The History of the Construction of the Moscow-Volga Canal

https://moskva-volga.ru/
A web site dedicated to the history of the construction of the Moscow-Volga Canal, a major Gulag construction project of the 1930s.

Virtual Museum of the Gulag

http://www.gulagmuseum.org
Compiled by the St. Petersburg, Russia, branch of "Memorial," it is a virtual collection of materials related to the history of the Gulag and Soviet terror.

Index

Figures and boxes are indicated by an italic *f* and *b* following the para ID.

N

O

COMMUNISM
A Very Short Introduction
Leslie Holmes

The collapse of communism was one of the most defining
moments of the twentieth century. At its peak, more than a
third of the world's population had lived under communist
power. What is communism? Where did the idea come from
and what attracted people to it? What is the future for
communism? This Very Short Introduction considers these
questions and more in the search to explore and understand
communism. Explaining the theory behind its ideology, and
examining the history and mindset behind its political,
economic and social structures, Leslie Holmes examines the
highs and lows of communist power and its future in today's
world.

Very readable and with its wealth of detail a most valuable
reference book.

Gwyn Griffiths, Morning Star

GLOBAL ECONOMIC HISTORY

A Very Short Introduction

Robert C. Allen

Why are some countries rich and others poor? In 1500, the income differences were small, but they have grown dramatically since Columbus reached America. Since then, the interplay between geography, globalization, technological change, and economic policy has determined the wealth and poverty of nations. The industrial revolution was Britain's path breaking response to the challenge of globalization. Western Europe and North America joined Britain to form a club of rich nations by pursuing four polices-creating a national market by abolishing internal tariffs and investing in transportation, erecting an external tariff to protect their fledgling industries from British competition, banks to stabilize the currency and mobilize domestic savings for investment, and mass education to prepare people for industrial work.

Together these countries pioneered new technologies that have made them ever richer. Before the Industrial Revolution, most of the world's manufacturing was done in Asia, but industries from Casablanca to Canton were destroyed by western competition in the nineteenth century, and Asia was transformed into 'underdeveloped countries' specializing in agriculture. The spread of economic development has been slow since modern technology was invented to fit the needs of rich countries and is ill adapted to the economic and geographical conditions of poor countries. A few countries - Japan, Soviet Russia, South Korea, Taiwan, and perhaps China - have, nonetheless, caught up with the West through creative responses to the technological challenge and with Big Push industrialization that has achieved rapid growth through investment coordination. Whether other countries can emulate the success of East Asia is a challenge for the future.

www.oup.com/vsi

RUSSIAN LITERATURE
A Very Short Introduction
Catriona Kelly

Rather than a conventional chronology of Russian literature, Catriona Kelly's Very Short Introduction explores the place and importance of literature of all sorts in Russian culture. How and when did a Russian national literature come into being? What shaped its creation? How have the Russians regarded their literary language? At the centre of the web is the figure of Pushkin, 'the Russian Shakespeare', whose work influenced all Russian writers, whether poets or novelists, and many great artists in other areas as well.

'brilliant and original, taking an unexpected approach to the subject, and written with great confidence and clarity.'

Peter France, University of Edinburgh

'a great pleasure to read. It is a sophisticated, erudite, searching, and subtle piece of work. It is written in a lively and stimulating manner, and displays a range to which few of Dr Kelly's peers in the field of Russian scholarship can aspire.'

Phil Cavendish, School of Slavonic and East European Studies, University of London

THE SOVIET UNION
A Very Short Introduction
Stephen Lovell

Almost twenty years after the Soviet Unions' end, what are we to make of its existence? Was it a heroic experiment, an unmitigated disaster, or a viable if flawed response to the modern world? Taking a fresh approach to the study of the Soviet Union, this Very Short Introduction blends political history with an investigation into the society and culture at the time. Stephen Lovell examines aspects of patriotism, political violence, poverty, and ideology; and provides answers to some of the big questions about the Soviet experience.

www.oup.com/vsi

THE FIRST WORLD WAR
A Very Short Introduction
Michael Howard

By the time the First World War ended in 1918, eight million people had died in what had been perhaps the most apocalyptic episode the world had known. This *Very Short Introduction* provides a concise and insightful history of the 'Great War', focusing on why it happened, how it was fought, and why it had the consequences it did. It examines the state of Europe in 1914 and the outbreak of war; the onset of attrition and crisis; the role of the US; the collapse of Russia; and the weakening and eventual surrender of the Central Powers. Looking at the historical controversies surrounding the causes and conduct of war, Michael Howard also describes how peace was ultimately made, and the potent legacy of resentment left to Germany.

'succinct, comprehensive and beautifully written. Indeed reading it is an experience comparable to scanning the clues of a well-composed crossword puzzle. Every allusion is eventually supplied with an answer, and the finished product defies the puzzler's disbelief that the intricacies can be brought to a convincing conclusion.... Michael Howard is the master of the short book'

TLS

www.oup.com/vsi

GEOPOLITICS
A Very Short Introduction
Klaus Dodds

In certain places such as Iraq or Lebanon, moving a few
feet either side of a territorial boundary can be a matter of life
or death, dramatically highlighting the connections between
place and politics. For a country's location and size as well as
its sovereignty and resources all affect how the people that live
there understand and interact with the wider world. Using
wide-ranging examples, from historical maps to James Bond
films and the rhetoric of political leaders like Churchill and
George W. Bush, this Very Short Introduction shows why,
for a full understanding of contemporary global politics, it is
not just smart - it is essential - to be geopolitical.

'Engrossing study of a complex topic.'

Mick Herron, Geographical.